John Christie:

The True Story of The Rillington Place Strangler

by Jack Rosewood

Historical Serial Killers and Murderers
True Crime by Evil Killers
Volume 17

Copyright © 2016 by Wiq Media

ALL RIGHTS RESERVED

No part of this book may be reproduced, stored in a retrieval system, or transmitted in any form or by any means, electronic, mechanical, photocopying, recording, scanning, or otherwise, without the prior written permission of the publisher.

ISBN-13:978-1533523341

DISCLAIMER:

This serial killer biography tells the story of one of Britain's worst serial killers, John Reginald Halliday Christie. It is not the intention of the author to defame or intentionally harm anyone involved. The interpretation of the events leading up to the discovery of the murders, are the opinion of the author as a result of researching this true crime killer. Any comments made about the motive and behavior of John Christie is the sole opinion and responsibility of the author.

Free Bonus!

Get two free books when you sign up to my VIP newsletter at www.jackrosewood.com
150 interesting trivia about serial killers
and the story of serial killer Herbert Mullin.

Contents

Introduction 1

CHAPTER 1: Christie's Childhood 4

    The Importance of His Grandfather's Death 5

CHAPTER 2: Becoming an Adult 7

    War Veteran 8

CHAPTER 3: Marriage to Ethel 9

    Sexual Dysfunction 10

CHAPTER 4: Early Criminal Career 12

    Where Did It All Go Wrong? 13

CHAPTER 5: John the Special Constable 15

    For The Love of Gas 16

CHAPTER 6: Timothy and Beryl Evans 18

    The Disappearance of Beryl and Geraldine 22

CHAPTER 7: Timothy Evans on Trial 25

    Witness Statements 26

    Crown Witness 28

    Judgement and Sentence 29

CHAPTER 8: The First Murders 31

Subsequent Murders 32

A Narrow Escape 37

Necrophilia 38

CHAPTER 9: Discovery of the Bodies 41

The Autopsies of Four 44

The Skeletal Remains 46

CHAPTER 10: Christie on the Run 47

The Confession 48

CHAPTER 11: The Trial 54

Psychiatric Evaluation 57

Christie's Trial Begins 58

Conviction and Execution 62

CHAPTER 12: The Aftermath 64

Demolition of 10 Rillington Place 64

Was Timothy Innocent? 66

Compensation for the Family 68

Judicial Failures Identified 69

CHAPTER 13: Personality Disorder? 72

Narcissistic Personality Disorder 73

Low Self-Confidence – Due to His Mother? 76

Sexual Dysfunction 77

CHAPTER 14: Were There More Victims? 81

    Questions Unanswered 86

    The Tobacco Tin..86

    Why Ethel Stayed 88

CHAPTER 15: In the Media... 90

Conclusion 92

A Note From The Author 132

Introduction

A dapper looking man with a haughty attitude and speaking voice hid a very indecent secret. John Reginald Halliday Christie became infamous for killing at least eight victims and stashing four of them within the confines of his flat. A sexually dysfunctional man with no care or respect for the lives of women, John was able to conceal his abhorrent actions for more than ten years.

During pre-and post-war London, the streets surrounding John's residence at 10 Rillington Place provided him with the supply of victims he so desperately craved. The women of the streets, the night walkers, the desperate, all were potential targets for John Christie. After all, nobody would miss them, would they? Their husbands had either gone to war and never came back, or perhaps they had never married in the first place. If they had been married, they wouldn't be out on the streets selling their bodies to provide a bed for the night or food to eat.

The 1940s and 1950s were a fairly dark period, and yet women were expected to maintain a high standard of morals. With no contraception available, many of these women of the streets found themselves in the terrible predicament of being pregnant. John saw this as an opportunity to try out his killing jar under the pretense of helping such women. He would claim that he knew how to perform abortions and invite them back to his flat. Desperate women will do desperate things, and those that followed him home were never seen again.

Not only did John commit these terrible murders, he also allowed an innocent man to die in his place. The story of Timothy Evans is heartbreaking, having lost his wife and his baby daughter, and to then be charged for the baby's murder. Sentenced to death, it would take many years for the truth to come out, but it was far too late. Timothy Evans had been sent to the gallows, partly due to the testimony given to the court by John Christie—the very man who later would be blamed for the murders of the baby and Timothy's wife Beryl.

The story of John Reginald Halliday Christie is sad and twisted, from murder, sexual dysfunction and perversion, and the grandiose feelings of superiority he felt. For a man who was struggling financially, who lived in absolute squalor following the murder of his own wife, and who was incapable of making friends, it is incredible that he still put on the act of being better than what he was. Yet underlying all of this was a history of female domination and low self-esteem. Mother dearest was overprotective, his sisters ruled the house, and his father was a stern disciplinarian. Could this have contributed to what John was to become? Or was he 'just not right' in the head to start with?

John Christie was executed a month after he was sentenced to death, as was the normal practice in England at that time. If there had have been a delay, could John have confessed to further murders? And why when he was captured was he carrying a newspaper article about the trial of Timothy Evans, so many years after the fact? Was he feeling guilt, or was he simply not capable of feeling empathy?

The trial of John opened up a lot more questions, some of which may never be answered. Accusations of police misconduct and malpractice, the truth regarding the innocence of Timothy Evans, and why John's wife Ethel stayed with him so long are some of those questions covered within the chapters of this book. By the time you have finished reading this book, you may even have answered some of the other questions yourself!

CHAPTER 1:
Christie's Childhood

On April 8, 1899, Ernest John Christie and his wife Mary Hannah Halliday welcomed their sixth child into the world near Halifax in the UK. This child would become known as John Reginald Halliday Christie, and little did they know that name would become famous for all the wrong reasons.

John's father, Ernest, worked as a carpet designer for a local factory. He was known to be a rather cold man who showed very little emotion, if any at all, and was largely uncommunicative to others. He ruled with an iron fist, and any perceived indiscretions or misbehaviors by his children were rewarded with punishments.

There would come to be seven children in all in the Christie family, with John being the only male child. This led to the household being dominated by the females in the family, as John and his father were very outnumbered by the fairer sex. John's mother was overprotective of him, and this, combined with the domination by his sisters, led to John having issues with self-esteem.

John was referred to as a bit of a 'queer lad' who kept to himself and wasn't popular with other children. What friendships he did make were short-lived, and he was often the subject of ridicule among his peers for a number of reasons. However, John was a very good student with an IQ of 128, and when he was eleven years old he won a scholarship to the Halifax Secondary School where he excelled at algebra and mathematics and performed in the church choir.

As a member of the Boy Scouts, John raised to the rank of scoutmaster by the time he was in his mid-teens. He had mentioned to others that he liked wearing the Boy Scout uniform, possibly because it gave him a sense of power, something he definitely did not have in his home life.

The Importance of His Grandfather's Death

When John was 8 years old, his grandfather passed away, and this would have a lasting impression on John, but not in the way the death of a close relative would normally cause. His parents gave him the option of seeing his grandfather's body laid out ready for the funeral and wake. John said yes, and when he looked at the body of his grandfather, something changed inside of him. He had always known his grandfather as a frightening man, and now he no longer felt any sense of fear emanating from the body. He was no longer scared of this man, and it intrigued him.

He was so fascinated by the response his mind had at seeing his dead grandfather that he started to spend time playing in the graveyard. He was drawn to the broken vaults, especially those which contained deceased children, and he would peer down between the cracks to see if he could see anything.

It was from this experience that John learned that there was nothing to fear from dead bodies. In fact, he felt a complete sense of peace and calm when viewing the deceased. This is when he began to associate death with pleasure.

CHAPTER 2:
Becoming an Adult

When John left school at the age of fifteen, he began working as an assistant projectionist at the local cinema. By then it was known among his peers that he had issues with the act of sex. He had failed to carry out the act of intercourse during his first few attempts, and as word got around about his difficulties he was subjected to nicknames like 'Reggie No Dick' and 'Can't Do It Christie'. These names would follow him right through his adolescence and into his early adulthood.

A slightly odd looking appearance didn't help things for John either. His hair was ginger in color and his eyes a very pale blue, but what stood out the most was that he seemed to have a very large forehead. He had developed into a hypochondriac, constantly feigning illnesses to gain attention. John had an overwhelming need for attention and to control those around him. Again, this is most likely due to his home life, growing up in a house full of women and a very domineering father.

War Veteran

When World War I broke out, John didn't hesitate to enlist and do his duty for his country. He enlisted as an infantryman and then a signalman, and there have been no reports of any real problems during his time in the Army.

However, when he was discharged from the Army, John claimed that he had been the victim of a mustard gas attack. Mustard gas was used all the time during the war as a form of chemical warfare, and it's true that many soldiers came back from the war changed and damaged because of it.

During his hospitalization for the mustard gas attack, John claimed to have lost his sight, but this has never been confirmed and was never recorded. Obviously he wasn't blind, as he went on to live his life without too much difficulty. Another effect of the gas, he claimed, was that he had lost the ability to speak at a normal volume. This was diagnosed as hysterical muteness, and it lasted for three years, during which time his voice was barely above a whisper.

Many believe that the muteness was false, and that John had feigned this illness like many others before. He did have a history of hypochondria, and so the belief was that he faked the muteness to gain attention and, to some degree, sympathy.

CHAPTER 3:
Marriage to Ethel

John had been introduced to Ethel Waddington Simpson from Sheffield, and on May 10, 1920, they married at the Registry Office. The marriage would be fraught with sexual dysfunction and criminal behavior. They separated just four years after the wedding, and John moved to London.

However, they were to reconcile quite a number of years later, around 1934, after John had done many stints in prison. Ethel and John decided to move into a new home in 1937, and they took up residence at 10 Rillington Place, in the flat on the top floor. Rillington Place was located in a fairly run-down part of London called Ladbroke Grove.

By December of 1938, they had shifted downstairs to the ground floor flat, which had a living room unlike the flat upstairs. The conditions within this 3-story brick building were considered to be squalid, with just one bathroom outside for all of the occupants to use. There were no indoor bathrooms or facilities, with the flats consisting of a bedroom, kitchen, and living room only.

The building at 10 Rillington Place was near part of the Metropolitan train line that happened to be above ground level. The sheer noise of the trains rushing past would have been deafening for any of the nearby residents, including John and Ethel. Yet, they settled into this home and went about their daily lives.

Sexual Dysfunction

John had always suffered from impotence, even during his adolescence, and this took a toll on the relationship between himself and Ethel. His issues went back to his childhood, at the time when he felt himself attracted to his domineering sisters. In John's head, they taunted him with their bodies and made him aroused, and then dominated him by bossing him around. In one moment, he both wanted them sexually and hated them at the same time.

The issues with his sisters went on every single day for years. His sisters didn't do anything wrong, however; it was all in John's head. John developed a great detest for women, and the more he failed at intercourse with them, the worse his hatred grew. For him it was all their fault that he couldn't perform.

From the young age of nineteen years, John began to take advantage of the services of prostitutes, and this continued throughout his relationship with Ethel. He seemed capable of performing to a degree with prostitutes, but could not do so with any woman he was in a relationship with. Perhaps he felt that paying a woman for sex made him the one in control.

CHAPTER 4:
Early Criminal Career

Throughout the decade following John's marriage to Ethel, he was arrested and convicted of a number of crimes, many of which resulted in him going to prison. The first crime he was arrested for was theft of postal orders while he was a postman. On the April 12, 1921, he was sentenced to three months in prison.

His next charge was for obtaining money by false pretenses and violence, and he received twelve months' probation in January of 1923. John had traveled down the path of theft, and this charge was the first violent charge against him. During the year 1924, he committed another two larceny crimes, and from September of that year he received a total of nine months' imprisonment.

Following his latest stint in prison, he moved to Battersea and was living with a known prostitute. He was subsequently arrested and convicted of assault against this prostitute and was sentenced to six months hard labor in May 1929. This crime was his most violent to date, as he had bashed her over the head using a cricket bat. Even the magistrate had called it a 'murderous' attack, and in later years it would prove to have been the start of the terror that was yet to come.

The next criminal act didn't take place until 1933. At the time, he had become friendly with a priest, and after stealing his car he was charged and convicted of theft and sentenced to another three months in prison. It's quite extraordinary that all of these crimes had resulted in rather short prison sentences.

Hindsight is a tremendous thing, and it would be many years before anyone realized that the assault against the prostitute could well have been his first attempt towards murder. His hatred of women and taste for prostitutes were all prerequisites for the majority of the murders he was to commit in the future.

Where Did It All Go Wrong?

It's quite unusual for a person to suddenly start committing crimes later in life. Usually, if a criminal is habitual, they would normally start off with petty crimes in their youth. John however, didn't start to get into trouble with the law until after he was married. He was around 22 years of age when he committed his first crime, and there was nothing in his background as a child that would have predicted that type of behavior.

Occasionally, crime can be an act of necessity or survival, especially during terrible financial times and economic crises. But there is no record of John being destitute or starving during this period of time. He had somewhere to live, a wife at home, and a job. So why did he start down this criminal path?

Perhaps the Christies were struggling to make ends meet, or maybe Ethel was a little more demanding than people knew. These reasons could certainly explain the theft and larceny. The assault against the prostitute is a completely different situation, however, and with what we know now, we can certainly assume that this was his first foray into acting on his hatred of women.

CHAPTER 5:
John the Special Constable

World War II started in 1939 and London was thrown into political turmoil. Having served in the army during World War I, John immediately sought to enlist to help, so he volunteered to be a member of what was called the War Reserve Police. Surprisingly, they did not delve into his past criminal record. If they had, he certainly would have been rejected for service.

John became a Special Constable, based at the Harrow Road Police Station, and he remained there for the next four years. It was the longest lasting job he had until then, and it seems as though he truly enjoyed it. This is probably due to once again being in a uniform and having the sense of power over others that came from it.

He loved his role as Special Constable so much that he became quite obsessive about upholding the law, and the locals gave him the nickname the 'Himmler of Rillington Place', in reference to the notorious German military figure. There was a darker side to John's legal diligence, and he abused the power and knowledge that came with the uniform.

John began to follow various women under the guise of doing his job, and he kept notes on these women which were found many years later. He also drilled a hole in his kitchen door to use as a peephole to monitor his neighbors. This peeping tom type activity was to remain unnoticed, which is a shame, as it may have been a very good clue of the type of man he really was.

His role as Special Constable came to an end at the end of 1943, following his resignation. It is not known why he gave up a job he clearly loved so much, especially considering his need to dominate and exert some sort of power over others. But resign he did, and he subsequently took a job at a radio factory as a clerk. It wouldn't be until many years later that it was discovered John had committed his first murder shortly before he resigned, and perhaps this was his reasoning for leaving his job as Special Constable.

For The Love of Gas

For some strange reason, John had developed a love of using gas under the guise of providing backstreet medical treatment. He claimed it could cure bronchitis, a lure that worked on one of his victims. He also claimed he had gained medical knowledge while working as a Special Constable, and could therefore perform abortions. At that time in England abortions were highly illegal, and women who sought them were considered to be dirty or of ill repute.

It's quite possible that John did perform abortions from time to time, especially given his association with prostitutes. Contraception was barely successful, and many of these street ladies found themselves in the predicament of being pregnant. How John came to be aware of gas as a way of rendering a person unconscious, or how he was able to get the necessary supplies, is a mystery. But the gas would play a pivotal part in the murders that were yet to come.

CHAPTER 6:
Timothy and Beryl Evans

Timothy and Beryl Evans were a young married couple expecting their first baby, who moved into 10 Rillington Place in 1948. They hadn't been married for long, only a year, and Timothy was twenty-four years old at the time and Beryl just nineteen years of age. The couple met each other through a blind date, and within weeks they had become engaged and shortly thereafter got married. At first they lived with Timothy's mother and his sisters, but when Beryl became pregnant, there was just not enough space in the home to raise the baby as well. Therefore, they found themselves moving into the flat on the top floor above John and Ethel.

Timothy was borderline mentally retarded, with an IQ of just 70. He had very little in the way of education due to difficulties with his behavior as a child and a foot injury that required multiple admissions to hospital. He had grown up in a South Wales mining town called Merthyr Tydfil, and his father had abandoned the family before Timothy was born.

He reportedly suffered shocking tantrums when he was a child, and he had a tense relationship with his mother and her later husband. He was known to be a habitual liar and tended to create fantasy situations that made him look better than he was. As a fairly small man, just five foot five inches tall and only weighing around 140 pounds, it is no wonder he tried to make himself out to be something he wasn't. Being small, uneducated, and prone to violent outbursts, Timothy was very difficult to deal with as a child and a young man.

Not a great deal is known about Beryl other than she was very petite and was considered to be as mentally immature as Timothy. She had developed a good relationship with Timothy's sisters, and they tried to help her whenever they could. Beryl had no mother in her life, so she leaned on Timothy's family for support. When they moved into Rillington Place, her housekeeping skills were very poor and she struggled to manage their finances, which were meager at best.

Of note, Timothy's sister Eileen was the one who located the flat for them and helped them to not only furnish the flat, but also to decorate it so it was more like a home. She recalled meeting the new neighbor, John Christie, and after that initial meeting she had concerns about his intentions towards women. He had entered the flat of Timothy and Beryl while Eileen was there without her knowledge, as though he had crept in silently, and all of a sudden was standing there next to her with a cup of tea in his hand. He offered it to her, and she turned it down, yet it seemed he had no intention of leaving. She told him Timothy would be back soon, and that seemed to work as John left.

Their first baby came along and they called her Geraldine. With the arrival of the baby came an increase in bills, and Timothy's wages were not enough to cover all of the costs. Beryl struggled as a mother and at times was thought to neglect her baby. This, coupled with her inability to cook and clean, led to many fights between Beryl and her husband. These were loud and sometimes violent arguments, and they were known to have struck each other on occasion out of anger. Timothy was fond of alcohol, and this further fueled his temper, and the arguments and disputes increased.

Beryl was under the impression in August of 1949 that Timothy would soon be heading overseas for work. Not wanting to be alone in the flat with the baby, she invited her 17 year-old friend Lucy Endecott to come and stay with them. She soon discovered that Timothy wasn't going anywhere, and for a while he was forced to sleep on the floor while Beryl shared the marital bed with Lucy.

Lucy began to come between Timothy and Beryl, and the fights got even worse. Many of these arguments were because of Lucy, so Timothy's mother forced her to leave their apartment.

Timothy was so angry that he threatened to throw Beryl out of the top story window, but instead he moved into another flat with Lucy. This didn't last very long though, probably because Lucy had found out just how violent he was, so he returned to Beryl at the flat in Rillington Place. Beryl took him back, goodness knows why, and Timothy visited all his friends voicing threats towards Lucy.

Things just got worse and worse for Beryl. Timothy had become even more violent towards her and at one point had tried to strangle her. Beryl didn't hesitate to tell his mother about this assault, but still Beryl stayed with Timothy. Before long, Beryl found out that once again she was pregnant. They were already living in squalid conditions with no money, and Beryl felt there was no choice but to try and get rid of the unborn baby.

There weren't a lot of options at that time to deal with unwanted pregnancies, but Beryl was able to get hold of some pills and douches to try and induce miscarriage, but they were unsuccessful. Timothy couldn't understand why she was so worried about having another baby, probably due to his low intelligence. The financial mess they were in seemed to be nothing to be worried about as far as Timothy was concerned, and he couldn't see why she would give up a pregnancy and carry on working to pay the bills.

But Beryl was determined to be rid of the pregnancy, and she was quick to tell other people about her wishes. Naturally she also told her neighbours, John and Ethel Christie. She could not see how they could possibly afford to raise another child, but abortions were illegal, so trying to find someone to do it for her would have been very difficult.

The Disappearance of Beryl and Geraldine

On November 8, 1948, Timothy came home to find his wife and baby daughter missing. John approached him and informed him that he had performed an abortion on Beryl, and there had been a complication. He claimed she had developed septic poisoning during the other methods of termination she had tried, and she had subsequently died during the abortion procedure. Being of such low intelligence, Timothy was easily convinced that rather than reporting the death to the police, he should go and stay with an aunt in Wales for a while.

He even believed that John knew of a couple who would take care of Geraldine while he was away. Most people would have asked questions, or at least demanded to see their baby and dead wife. But Timothy wasn't like most people and perhaps was in a state of shock, and he never questioned what John was saying to him.

However, Timothy's mother was perplexed about the disappearance of Beryl and Geraldine, and questioned Timothy about it. That confrontation between mother and son on November 30 led to Timothy going to the police station in Merthyr Tydfil and reporting that his wife was dead.

At first, in an act of trying to protect John, Timothy confessed that he had accidentally killed Beryl by giving her pills to cause an abortion. He also claimed he had gotten rid of her body by placing her in a sewer drain. The police investigated the drain right away, but of course found nothing. Timothy was interrogated again in a more intense manner, and he cracked and admitted he had lied and that John was involved in Beryl's death.

The police returned to the Rillington Place flat and searched again for signs of Beryl and Geraldine. When they still couldn't locate them, the ventured outside and began to search the backyard area. They approached the laundry room and tried to enter, but the door was stuck shut. Ethel Christie, always the kind hearted helper, gave the police officers a piece of metal to try and pry the door open with. The door opened, but they could see very little in the dark room.

The officers noticed some wood leaning up against the sink in the laundry room, and when reaching behind the wood an officer touched something, so they moved the wood out of the way. Behind it was an object wrapped up in a tablecloth and tied up with some cord. Ethel denied having ever seen it before and had no idea what it could be.

The wrapped object was pulled out further and untied. To their shock, two feet slipped out of the wrapping and the dead body of Beryl was discovered. They searched the laundry room further and located the tiny body of Geraldine beneath some other wood that was behind the door. On initial inspection, both Beryl and Geraldine had been strangled, with a man's necktie still tied around the Geraldine's neck.

CHAPTER 7:
Timothy Evans on Trial

Despite having already claimed that John had been involved in the death of Beryl during an illegal abortion operation, Timothy eventually confessed to having killed her himself. There has been some controversy about this confession, with many people believing it was a false confession concocted by the police.

As soon as he was charged with the murder, Timothy immediately withdrew his confession and claimed once again that John had killed Beryl. By now though, Timothy had gone back and forth between blaming John and confessing so many times that anything he said now was not taken seriously. He was subsequently put on trial for the murder of Geraldine on January 11, 1950. He was never charged with the murder of Beryl, as it was considered that Geraldine's death was the more heinous crime and one for which he was likely to be judged more harshly.

The trial took place at the famous Old Bailey in London, and though he wasn't charged for Beryl's death, the circumstances of her murder were included in the testimony. The presiding judge was Mr. Justice Lewis, who was not well at the time, and the prosecutor was a man named Christmas Humphreys. Incredibly, the case of the prosecutor relied on the testimony of John Christie as the chief witness! This seems completely bizarre, considering John had been accused numerous times by Timothy of being the murderer!

The main reason for prosecuting Geraldine's death and not Beryl's was because the murder of Beryl could be construed as being due to provocation, and therefore the charge could be reduced to manslaughter. The motive for Geraldine's murder however could not be considered the same, with it instead being more cold-blooded, and therefore the charge would not be reduced from murder.

The legal firm initially acting on behalf of Timothy was Freeborough, Slack, and Company, but they did not follow through, failing to investigate. Their assumption that Timothy was indeed guilty resulted in important witnesses not being called, and no investigation into John's criminal record was undertaken. If these things had been followed up on, the jury may have been forced to consider reasonable doubt.

Witness Statements

The initial statement taken from Ethel Christie by the police was ridiculously improbable. She claimed that she always got her household water from the very laundry room the bodies were found in every single day. If this was true, then on the more than two dozen occasions she had entered the small room to get the water, surely she would have noticed the smell. A decaying body emits a putrid smell, and it is the type of scent that is not likely to go unnoticed. There was also a dog on the property, and she claimed the dog had never picked up on an odor either. Interestingly, when she was brought before the court as a witness, Ethel changed her story, claiming she never went into the laundry room at all. Yet, nobody noticed this discrepancy in her statements.

A carpenter by the name of Anderson had been brought in to do repairs on the property at Rillington Place, and he was called as a witness because of the wood that had been used to conceal the bodies of Beryl and Geraldine. He constantly contradicted himself throughout his testimony and changed his story seemingly to fit the crown's case. At one point he claimed he had pulled the wood out of the floor on November 11, but he later changed this statement to suit the dates of the deaths given by the police. He still got it wrong, because he hadn't given the wood to John until three days after the 11th, so that would have made it the 14th, long after the murders. A time sheet for the carpenter's work that had been given to the police disappeared from the file, and it turns out this was the only document that did go missing.

Timothy had stated to the attorney defending John that he was convinced the police would beat him if he didn't confess to the murders, thereby suggesting coercion by threats of violence. This information would have been useful for his defense based on the false confession, and although the attorney, Morris, felt that the case wouldn't successfully pin the crime on John, Timothy was so persistent that he agreed to try to convince the judge and jury.

Crown Witness

The crown witness in this case was John. He appeared on the stand, and first impressions were that he was a pleasant, well-mannered man who referred to himself as a victim and a hero. His demeanor was such that it deeply contrasted with the seemingly crazed picture Timothy presented of himself. John spoke quietly and took the time to consider each question before he answered it. He ensured the jury and the judge knew of his service during the wars and the physical disabilities (as he perceived them) he suffered as a result of serving his country.

The way he answered the questions gave the appearance of a man who was trying to help as much as possible, by pondering what was asked and trying to give as much detail as possible. Towards the end of his testimony, Morris discovered the truth about John's criminal past, and brought that up for John to answer to. Unfortunately, this backfired because John hadn't been arrested for seventeen years, so it seemed as though the man who had once been bad had turned his life around for the good. This impressed the jury even further!

Judgement and Sentence

The instructions given by the judge to the jury at the end of the case were given in such a way that it was almost as good as if he had said straight out that Timothy was guilty. He reminded them that the charge was the murder of Geraldine, and that there were no charges for Beryl's murder. He completely ignored statements from the case that could create an air of reasonable doubt, and he even reminded the jury panel that despite his early criminal behavior, John had been completely clean from any crime for such a long time. The history of lying by Timothy was also brought to the jurors' attention again by the judge. Many felt that the sarcastic way in which the judge summed up the case had more or less been an instruction to the jury to find Timothy guilty.

Not surprisingly, following that summation by the judge, the jury took just forty minutes to reach their verdict. Timothy was found guilty of the murder of his daughter Geraldine and sentenced to death. On hearing the sentence of death, John began to cry.

Timothy never wavered from his final statements that John had killed Beryl and Geraldine for the rest of his days. He did make an attempt to appeal the conviction and sentence, but this failed. Back in those days, the time spent in jail before execution was very short, and on March 9, 1950, only a couple of months after the trial, he was hanged.

CHAPTER 8:
The First Murders

John's killing spree started in 1943, and to date there have been eight known murder victims, though it is highly suspected that there were more.

Ruth Fuerst

Ruth Fuerst was just twenty-one years of age when her path crossed with John Christie on August 16, 1943. She was an Austrian migrant who was working in a munitions factory. Trying to make ends meet, she was also working as a prostitute part time. According to John, he met Ruth in Ladbroke Grove while she was trying to solicit clients in a snack bar. He invited her back to his home, as Ethel was away, and while they were having sex he strangled her. Initially he hid her body beneath the floorboards of the living room, but he later moved her and buried her in the back garden.

Muriel Amelia Eady

Since resigning as a Special Constable, John had found employment at a radio factory as a clerk, and in 1944 this would bring him into contact with his second victim. Muriel Amelia Eady was 32 years old and supposedly suffered from bronchitis, a breathing disorder. John had convinced her that he had a method of curing bronchitis, and therefore lured her back to his home. Once again Ethel was away, so he could carry out his plan without interference. The concoction he claimed to have created to cure the bronchitis was in fact Friar's Balsam, which was only really used to hide the smell of the gas he would get her to inhale. He sat her on a chair and placed a tube into the jar containing the Friar's Balsam, and as she inhaled he stood behind her and connected a second tube to the gas tap. Before long she became unconscious, as the gas used in those days contained a high level of carbon monoxide. John raped Muriel and then killed her by strangulation. Her body was buried in the back garden near Ruth Fuerst's.

Subsequent Murders

By now John had also murdered Beryl Evans and Geraldine Evans, bringing the total number of victims to four. But he wasn't finished yet, and there would be at least another four to come.

Ethel Christie

On December 6, 1952, John had resigned from his job. On the 14th of that same month, John murdered his wife Ethel, strangling her while she was still in bed. He placed her body beneath the floorboards of the parlor, wrapped in a blanket. Ethel was 54 years old and had been with John on and off for most of her adult life. John had been unable to find further work since resigning from his job, and to support himself he began to sell various items in the home, including Ethel's wedding ring. He concocted a number of different stories to explain away the disappearance of Ethel, including telling her relatives that she had rheumatism and could no longer write letters. To others he claimed she had gone away to visit relatives, which was plausible as she often did exactly that. Struggling financially on his unemployment benefits, he forged Ethel's signature and withdrew everything from her bank account on January 26, 1953.

Rita Nelson

Rita Nelson was a young blond woman from Ireland who had moved to London to live. At just twenty-five years old and without a husband, she found herself in the predicament of being pregnant. This was a terribly shameful position to be in, as unmarried mothers were socially frowned upon. Rita had gone to visit her sister who lived in Ladbroke Grove, and instead of visiting the hospital for an appointment about her pregnancy on January 19, 1953, she was sitting in the local pub drinking with her sister. John started chatting with Rita and couldn't help but notice her pregnancy, and on hearing about her distress over the situation, he offered to help her by performing an abortion.

Rita, willing to do anything to be rid of the pregnancy despite being around 24 weeks pregnant, followed John back to his flat in Rillington Place. It's surprising that the condition of the flat didn't put her off and make her run for the hills, as it was in a shockingly squalid state, and there was a putrid smell that no amount of disinfectant could hide. Still, she was a desperate woman. John offered her a chair in the kitchen and then produced the jar of liquid he had used before, and it is assumed he told her it was an anesthetic she needed to inhale. While she inhaled from the jar, he held the gas hose close to her face, and quickly she became unconscious. John then proceeded to rape her at the same time as strangling her to death using a cord.

With Ethel under the floorboards and the threat of being seen if he was to dig another hole in the backyard, John was faced with a difficult decision—where to dispose of Rita's body. He left her lying on the kitchen floor and went off to bed, planning on solving the issue in the morning. The next day, he decided that the most logical place to put Rita's body was in the small pantry hidden behind a cupboard. John placed a cloth over her head and tied it securely, then tied a cord around her ankles. Rita was dressed, and he placed a cloth between her legs and stood her upside down in the small pantry.

Kathleen Maloney

Kathleen Maloney was just twenty-six years old when her life would come to an end at the hands of John. She had experienced a difficult childhood as an orphan and ended up with five children of her own, despite there being no husband or regular partner. Kathleen had met John earlier in early December 1952, and at that time had joined him in a room with another prostitute whom John had taken naked photographs of. Therefore, when she ran into him again in February 1953, he probably didn't seem to be a threat. Kathleen and a friend had spent the day in a Notting Hill café drinking alcohol, and when John joined them, they were talking about looking for a new flat. Always the opportunist, John saw the chance to lure her back to his flat, most likely telling her there was an empty room there or that maybe he was moving and she could rent his flat. It's not known exactly what ruse he used, but whatever it was, it worked, and she willingly accompanied him home.

By this time Kathleen was rather intoxicated, and it was not too difficult for John to get her into the kitchen chair and gas her. Once she was unconscious, he tied a rope around her neck and strangled her to death as he raped her. She had been wearing a white vest, and he removed this and placed it between her legs and left her sitting in the chair overnight while he went to bed.

The following morning, he took a blanket and wrapped Kathleen's body in it, tying it around her feet with a sock. A pillowcase was placed over her head and tied in place using another sock. She was then placed into the pantry with Rita. For some unknown reason, John had tossed some ashes and dirt over Kathleen's body.

Hectorina MacLennan

John met 26-year-old Hectorina MacLennan at a café, and along with her boyfriend Alex Baker, she was practically homeless. Hectorina and Alex would sleep wherever they could find a spot to lie down, and after meeting a few times with John at the local pub they took up his offer of staying at his place until they could find a flat of their own. However, the state of John's flat put them off, with its lack of furniture and terrible smell, and after putting up with it for several days they left.

On March 6, 1953, John met up with Hectorina and Alex at the Labor Exchange while collecting his unemployment benefit. Somehow he managed to convince Hectorina to come back to his flat with him alone, without bringing Alex with her. Although it is not known what he said to convince her, the assumption is that he offered to pay her for sex, and being destitute and homeless, she most likely would have taken him up on his offer.

Unlike the other murders, this one would prove to be more difficult. John had given Hectorina a drink, and while he thought she was distracted he tried to place the gas tube near her head, but she became alarmed and ran from the kitchen. John quickly grabbed her and throttled her by the throat just enough to make her pass out. She was then put back into the kitchen chair, and he gassed her until she was unconscious completely. Then, placing her on the floor, he tied a piece of cord around her throat and strangled her as he raped her.

Hectorina's wrists were tied together using a handkerchief, and the only clothing on her was a sweater and white jacket, and these would become pushed up to her neck as he dragged her across the floor to the pantry cupboard. Her body was sat in the cupboard with her back towards the door, and to stop her from falling backwards he had hooked her bra onto the blanket used to cover Kathleen Maloney's legs.

It was not surprising that Alex came to John's flat looking for Hectorina, and even less of a surprise that John would lie and say he hadn't seen her. Alex was invited inside for a cup of tea, and despite noticing the terrible odor was still present in the flat, he left without suspecting John of killing his girlfriend.

A Narrow Escape

At least one woman is known to have escaped the deadly clutches of John Christie. Margaret Forrest had met John, and on hearing that she suffered terribly from migraines, he was sure he had met his next victim. Like others before, John claimed that he had the medical expertise to cure her of her affliction. He had even explained to her that he used coal gas to cure many medical problems, and for some bizarre reason these women believed him!

With a little persuasion, Margaret agreed to come to John's flat later to take him up on his offer of ridding her of migraines. However, she never arrived at his flat. John was livid that she hadn't bothered to show up, and knowing where she was staying, he made his way there to confront her. He demanded Margaret come to his flat immediately. She agreed to meet him there, but once again she failed to turn up. Apparently, she had actually lost his address—a lucky twist of fate, as it surely saved her life.

Necrophilia

There has been some debate for many years as to whether or not John was a necrophiliac. The confusion comes from misinformation, as many think that necrophilia only involves having sexual intercourse with a corpse. However, there are different forms of necrophilia, and in order to determine whether or not John fitted into this category, we need to work out whether he fits the profile or behavior patterns.

Fantasy Necrophilia:

For those with the propensity towards fantasy necrophilia, their erotic imagery surrounds death. A lover may be asked to pretend to be dead during the act of sex, and for others, they like to take photographs of their lovers 'looking' dead, so they can use these later for masturbation. Does John fit this behavior? In some ways, yes he does. He needed his victims to be unconscious before he had sex with them, and their unresponsiveness mimicked death.

Violent Necrophilia:

The violent necrophiliac will kill so they can be near a dead body and will often have sex with the corpse for a period of time. Often, once the body has been buried, they will return to the grave site multiple times to visit. Does this sound like John? No, not really. While it's true that he disposed of the bodies near him, there is no evidence that he continued to have sex with the bodies or that he visited them and spent time with them. Though when John relayed the death of Ruth Fuerst, he stated that as he pulled away from the body following sex, she was both urinary and fecally incontinent, which indicates that she had already passed away before he had finished raping her.

Romantic Necrophiliac:

Those that fit this category form a strong bond with their victims and will keep them near after their deaths. They don't necessary touch the corpse or perform sexual acts with the body, but they have a need to have them nearby. So, the important factor in romantic necrophilia is keeping the corpse around them, not the sexual perversion. Does John fit this category? It could be said that he does, as he certainly kept the bodies near, in his flat and his garden. But, it could be argued that he disposed of the bodies this way out of necessity rather than need. He may have been fearful of being caught if he tried to dispose of them elsewhere.

CHAPTER 9:
Discovery of the Bodies

John had met a Mrs. Reilly and invited her to his flat, supposedly because she was looking for somewhere to live, on March 20, just two weeks following the murder of Hectorina MacLennan. It's possible that he invited her so that he could kill again, but he didn't factor in that she may have a husband. When the couple arrived at his flat, he did offer it to them for rent. After all, the flat was in a terrible state. There was still the lingering smell coming from the decomposing bodies, and it was time for him to make his escape. Despite all of this, the Reilly's agreed to sublet the flat, and John packed his meager belongings and left.

That same evening, the landlord arrived to check on the flat and was shocked to find the Reilly's in residence. The subletting had been illegal, so they were given until the following morning to move out again. Meanwhile, he allowed Beresford Brown from the top-floor flat to use John's kitchen, as his wasn't useable. Four days later, on March 24, Brown set about trying to attach brackets to the wall so that he could place his radio. He knocked on the wall in several areas to find the right spot for attaching the brackets and noticed a hollow sounding area. Curious, he began to peel back the wallpaper and discovered a door that was closed securely. There was a slight crack in the door, and when he shone a light through it, he was shocked by what he had seen.

Right away Brown contacted the police, and because of the history of the murders of Beryl and Geraldine Evans, they immediately conducted a search of the whole property. On the scene were Chief Superintendent Peter Beveridge, Chief Inspector Percy Law of Scotland Yard, and a pathologist.

The initial search started at the site of the previously hidden cupboard. When they pried open the door, they saw a woman's body sitting with her back to them, with rubble at her feet. They could see behind her that there was another large object that was wrapped up in a blanket. The first body discovered was taken out of the cupboard and transferred to the front room so that an examination could be done and photographs taken. It was obvious that she had been strangled. The corpse was quite well preserved, probably due to the coolness in the cupboard.

The police shifted their attention to the other blanket-wrapped object in the cupboard, and as they were photographing it in situ, they noticed another similar object behind it. The second body was found to be upside down and propped up against the wall, and the body was moved out of the way. As suspected, they found the third object to be another female body, and all three corpses were taken to the morgue for further examination.

During the search of the flat, the officers noticed some loose floorboards in the parlor, largely because one of the officers had tripped on it! On removing the floorboards, they came across some rubble, and as they dug down beneath it, they found the fourth female body. This one was left in the flat overnight under police guard. On searching the back yard, the officers noticed a human femur (thigh bone) propped up against the wooden fence. Incredibly, despite being on the premises twice before following the deaths of Beryl and Geraldine Evans, they had never noticed the bone before! On digging in the garden, more bones were unearthed, some of which were blackened, probably from fire. Despite there only being one skull located in the back yard, the on-site pathologist determined that from the number of bones found there were two bodies buried there.

Some rather unusual objects were also discovered during the search. Under the floor of the common hall, they found a man's suit. It has never been explained why that suit was placed under the floorboards or who it may have belonged to. In a kitchen cupboard they located a man's neck tie that had been tied in a reef knot, the same type of knot used on the cords and bindings on the bodies. Perhaps the most disturbing discovery, aside from the bodies of course, was a tobacco tin that held a collection of pubic hair, later found to belong to four women. However, none of these hairs belonged to the women found in the cupboard. The hunt for John Christie began.

The Autopsies of Four

Four of the bodies, those found inside the flat, were autopsied at the mortuary. At that period in time, autopsies would have only been performed on reasonably preserved bodies, unlike the skeletal remains found in the garden.

Body Number 1:

The first body autopsied was a brunette woman aged around twenty-six years of age, although at first the coroner estimated her age to be only twenty years old. The coroner determined she had been deceased for around four weeks, and she had been poisoned by carbon monoxide and then strangled. There was evidence of a sexual assault taking place either shortly before she expired or immediately after. She also had marks on her back that suggested she had been dragged across the floor after death.

Body Number 2:

This female with light brown hair was estimated to be around twenty years of age. Her hands and feet were not manicured, and her skin was pink indicating carbon monoxide poisoning. She also had been strangled to death. Evidence showed that she had engaged in sexual intercourse around the time of her death. Her blood results also showed that she had consumed a lot of alcohol the day of her death. The time of death was estimated to have been between eight and twelve weeks earlier. This victim was still dressed in a vest and cardigan, and a white vest had been placed in between her legs.

Body Number 3:

Like body number two, this victim also had poorly manicured hands and feet. She was around twenty-five years of age and blond. She was fully dressed with a piece of cloth between her legs. Her skin was also pink in color, such as the hue that occurs with carbon monoxide poisoning. She had also been strangled and had consumed alcohol the same day as her death. This victim was six months pregnant.

Body Number 4:

The fourth victim was a lot older, in her 50s, and had many missing teeth. With this victim there were no signs of sexual intercourse or any type of gas poisoning. She had been strangled, more likely with a ligature rather than bare hands. It was automatically assumed that this victim was Ethel Christie.

Each of these victims was subsequently identified to be Ethel, Kathleen Maloney, Rita Nelson, and Hectorina MacLennan.

The Skeletal Remains

Although a full autopsy couldn't be performed on the skeletal remains found in the back yard, they were reconstructed so that as much information as possible could be gained, especially for identification purposes. One of the teeth found with a crown indicated that the victim was most likely from Austria or Germany. Her age was estimated at approximately twenty-one years, and she was quite tall, standing around 5 feet 7 inches.

The second set of remains was estimated to be older, between the ages of thirty-two and thirty-five years. This victim was also much shorter, standing around 5 feet 2 inches. The length of time they had both been dead was estimated as being somewhere between three and ten years. Nowadays of course, this could have been further specified, but the technology and knowledge available today certainly wasn't around back then.

Looking at missing persons, it was found the Ruth Margarete Fuerst fit the identifying markers on the first skeleton. The second skeleton was identified as Muriel Amelia Eady, and hair found in John's flat matched hair samples found on one of her dresses. The identifying markers matched her height, age, and coloring, and remnants of fabric found with her remains matched the description of what she had been wearing when she was last seen.

CHAPTER 10:
Christie on the Run

After leaving the flat on March 20, John booked a room for seven nights at Rowton House in King's Cross. Remarkably, he checked in under his own name and real address—a strange thing to do if you're a man on the run! He would only end up staying for four nights, and it is assumed that he had heard about the police hunting for him and so decided to go into hiding.

According to John, he wandered the streets of London after stashing his suitcase in a storage locker. He would sleep wherever he could, often on benches in parks or in darkened cinemas. A photograph of John wearing his raincoat had been released to the media, and so John bought a different coat from a man and gave him his overcoat. Later John would claim that he wandered around in a daze, and though he saw the newspaper headlines, he didn't associate the crimes with himself. However, if he was so dazed, how could he have had the sense to change his coat?

John quickly ran out of money and ended up wandering along the banks of the river Thames. On March 31, he was seen by a police officer, and when questioned about his identity John gave the officer a fake name and address. Police officers had been told about John's incredibly large forehead and to use it as an identifying factor. So, the officer asked John to remove his hat, and on doing so he identified him as the wanted man immediately.

When he was arrested, the officer searched his person to see what he may have been carrying. He found a ration book, his identity card showing he was John Christie, an ambulance badge, and his Union card. Oddly, he was also carrying a newspaper clipping about Timothy Evans and the murders of Beryl and Geraldine. Why he would be carrying this clipping could be explained by his guilt of sending an innocent man to the gallows for a crime he did not commit.

The Confession

John was taken to the Putney Police Station and interviewed. At first John refused to admit to committing the murders, but once he was told about the bodies found at his flat, he admitted to killing only the four found inside the house. During his time on the run, he hadn't kept up with case developments, so he was unaware they had also found the two in the garden. This is probably why he only confessed to the four, as he thought he might have gotten away with the other two. His confessions were almost absurd, as he tried to shift the blame to the women themselves.

John's Confession Regarding Ethel's Death

According to John, he had been woken during the night by Ethel flailing wildly in the bed, and it appeared to him she was choking. He claimed her face had turned a shade of blue, indicating that she couldn't get her breath, and because it was so late at night help was unable to be summoned. He felt the only thing he could do was put her out of her misery by strangling her with a stocking.

He then stated he had found his insomnia pills bottle and that it had been emptied. Therefore, he assumed Ethel had attempted to commit suicide with the pills because she didn't like the new tenants. According to John, the tenants were Jamaicans and Ethel believed they had been harassing her. In his grief, he left Ethel in bed for a few days before remembering the loose floorboards in the front room.

Wrapping Ethel's body in a blanket, he placed her beneath the floor to keep her nearby. John had tried to convince the police that this had been a 'mercy' killing, a form of kindness shown to his wife of so many years who was clearly suffering. They didn't fall for it. For all his 'cleverness', the damage was already done when the first thing he said was that he strangled a choking woman. This in itself was an admission of murder.

Rita Nelson's Death – According to John

To shift the blame from himself, John claimed that Rita Nelson had tried to extort money from him on the street. He said she threatened to make a scene by shouting that he had assaulted her if he didn't give her 30 shillings. John stated that he walked away from her, but she followed him back to his flat and forced her way in. He claimed she grabbed a frying pan and went to hit him with it, and a struggle ensued, during which time she fell backwards onto a chair. He remembers seeing a bit of rope on the chair but then claims he blacked out. When he regained consciousness, he found she had been strangled, and he claimed Rita accidentally did this to herself by landing on the rope.

The fact that he left her lying on the floor while he had a cup of tea and then went to bed certainly doesn't give the impression of a man who had just found a dead woman in his kitchen. It wasn't until the next morning that he wrapped her in the blanket and placed her in the cupboard.

John's Story of Kathleen Maloney's Death

His explanations of the deaths of these women got stranger and more ludicrous with each one. According to John, he had met Kathleen previously before Christmastime. After running into her again later, she told him that she was looking for a flat to live in. His story claimed that he told her he could put in a good word with his landlord, but this was clearly a lie because there were no rooms to rent at 10 Rillington Place at that time. John stated she made advances and he rebuffed her, and she threatened to do him harm. At this point he says his memory was fuzzy, just like with Rita's death, and when he awoke she was dead. He claimed he couldn't recall actually killing her. Like Rita, he wrapped her, tied her up, and placed her in the cupboard.

It Was Hectorina MacLennan's Fault

Once again John laid all the blame on the victim. He did admit that he had allowed Hectorina and her boyfriend to stay with him at the flat because they were desperate and homeless. His story was that after several days he had asked them to move on, and they did leave. But, he reckoned Hectorina came back the next night by herself, supposedly to wait for her boyfriend. John claimed he tried to get her to leave, and they ended up in a physical struggle. All of a sudden, she collapsed on the floor, and as she did so her clothing had become wrapped around her neck and strangled her. He dragged Hectorina into the kitchen and placed her on a chair, but she was clearly dead. Again, he wrapped the body and placed it into the cupboard with the others. This story was the most ridiculous of them all, and there were so many holes in it that it was insulting to the intelligence of the police officers that he expected them to believe him.

Up until now, the police had only given him tidbits of information that they knew or suspected about the murders. As far as John knew, they only had four bodies, but he was soon to find out that they knew about the others as well. When they informed him that they had found the other two bodies in the garden, he had to quickly come up with stories about those deaths as well.

Ruth Fuerst Brought It on Herself

He admitted that he knew Ruth was a prostitute and that he had used her services on several previous occasions. Whenever Ethel was away visiting relatives, Ruth would join John at the flat. Around August 24, 1943, they had been lying in bed when John received a telegram from Ethel stating she was coming home earlier than originally planned and that her brother would be accompanying her. This made Ruth declare her love for John and state that she wanted to be with John. She tried to seduce John by undressing (why was she dressed if they were in bed?) and begged John to leave his wife and be with her.

According to John, he turned her down but they still had intercourse, during which he strangled her. Initially he put her body under the floorboards in the front room, and because Ethel and her brother arrived, it would be another two days before he could move the body out to the back yard.

Muriel was Sexually Aggressive Toward John

If John's stories were to be believed, women were throwing themselves at him left, right, and center, which isn't really believable given that he wasn't the most attractive man around. His story about the death of Muriel Eady was very similar to his previous tales. According to John, Muriel had been aggressive sexually towards him, and out of fear of his wife learning of their affair, he killed her. After he had buried her in the back garden, at one point he had accidentally dug up the leg bone later found propping up the wooden fence. It wasn't until much later that he confessed that he had gassed her under the pretense of curing her bronchitis and then killed her during sexual intercourse.

CHAPTER 11:
The Trial

Before the trial could take place, further investigation into John's background and a psychiatric evaluation had to take place. On interviewing those who had known John since childhood, the police discovered the truth about his sexual dysfunctions and how he had been called a number of associated nicknames throughout his youth. Coupled with the female dominated household he grew up in, it didn't take the police long to come to the conclusion that John had been killing women to vent his hatred and rage upon them.

While awaiting his trial, John was held in Brixton Prison, and he certainly wasn't popular among his fellow inmates. He loved to brag about his crimes and likened himself to another well-known serial killer of the time, John George Haigh. He claimed that he had planned to outdo Haigh by killing more women than him, and that his goal was to murder twelve—double the body count of Haigh.

Eventually John admitted the truth about his method of using gas and the killing jar with the sedating concoction. The stories he now told about the deaths of Ruth Fuerst and Muriel Eady were much more plausible, and it seemed as though he was finally admitting everything about the murders.

He changed his initial story about the death of his wife Ethel, and the new version fitted much better with what evidence the police had. He also gave a lot more detail about the deaths of his last three victims, including how he had sex with each of them as he was strangling them to death. One point he emphasized was that he didn't have sex with any of the bodies after death, as he didn't want people to think he was a necrophiliac. What he didn't realize was that by having sex with them as they died, this was still a form of necrophilia.

The most shocking confession that John made was his admission of killing Beryl Evans back in 1949. The details he gave about the murder convinced the investigators that he was telling the truth. It is important to note here that while he was confessing to the murder, he was still trying to paint himself as the victim to gain sympathy rather than condemnation. Of course this failed.

Once his confession regarding the death of Beryl came out, there was a major attempt made by the justice system to have this information quashed or denied. After all, Beryl's husband Timothy had already been convicted and executed for the murder of the baby and Beryl's associated murder, and the Crown was trying to save face from the embarrassment and guilt of getting it so wrong. Throughout his confession however, John continued to deny murdering baby Geraldine, and it was this crime that Timothy was hanged for.

According to John, the murder of Beryl Evans was yet another mercy killing, a similar excuse he used when explaining his wife Ethel's death. His story was that he entered Beryl's flat and found her trying to kill herself with the coal gas. He alleged she was deeply depressed and distraught about being pregnant again and not having the means to support another mouth to feed. He claims he saved her from going through with the suicide, but that Beryl then begged him to help her finish the job. The following day, at her request, he went up to her flat and gassed her then strangled her because she had asked him to. He also alleged that Beryl had offered to pay him for his assistance with sex, but he was unable to perform. The confession of the murder of Beryl would later be recanted by John to the prison chaplain. However, his attorney felt it was better to keep the confession as it was due to his intended plea of insanity, rationalizing that the more murders there were, the more likely he would be deemed insane.

The matter of the tobacco tin containing pubic hair was investigated, but the owners of the hairs were never identified, except for those that came from Ethel. John had admitted some of the hairs had come from Ethel, and he claimed that others had been clipped from Beryl's body. To try and prove this one way or another, Beryl's body was exhumed and examined. However, there were no signs that any of her pubic hair had been cut, and subsequent tests showed that her hairs did not match any located in the tobacco tin.

In fact, the hairs in the tin did not match any of the bodies found at 10 Rillington Place. John claimed he couldn't recall where he had gotten the hairs from or from whom. It was possible some of them could have come from Ruth Fuerst and Muriel Eady, but this was unable to be proven as their remains had been reduced to skeletons, and no hairs could be found.

Psychiatric Evaluation

Suspecting correctly that John would plead an insanity defense, the Crown ordered a psychiatric evaluation to see if he was sane and fit to stand trial. It was going to be extremely difficult for his team to prove he was insane, as his actions were those of a sane man. By legal definition, a person who is insane does not recognize their deeds as being wrong. John, however, had the clearness of mind to hide evidence, attempted disguise by changing his overcoat, and attempted to fool the investigators. Therefore, these were not the actions of an insane man. Nevertheless, the evaluation had to be done.

When a psychiatric examination is done for legal purposes, as you would imagine, the job would not be easy or pleasant, as the psychiatrists are potentially talking to some of the worst people you could come across. Not one single psychiatrist who interviewed John liked him, with some referring to him as sniveling and nauseating. His stories were constantly changing, and each person he spoke to would receive a different version.

His tendency to whisper, supposedly from the mustard gas incident during the war, would vary depending on who he was talking to and whether or not he felt as though he was being confronted or being asked what he found to be uncomfortable questions. The doctors found that when he discussed the murders he had a dissociative quality and often referred to himself in the third-person. Some thought that his reasoning behind this act was to try to establish a diagnosis of split-personality disorder.

Despite all his attempts to convince the psychiatrists that he was insane, they were more astute than he thought, and every one of them determined him to be sane. Therefore he was culpable for his murderous crimes and fit to stand trial.

Christie's Trial Begins

The trial was set to take place at the infamous Old Bailey, on June 22, 1953. Ironically, the courtroom assigned to the case was the exact same one that Timothy Evans had been sentenced to death in earlier. The charge brought against John was of the murder of Ethel, as the prosecution team felt that was the one they had the most evidence for and therefore was likely to be the most successful. Charges for the murders of Kathleen, Hectorina, and Rita were also laid against John, but these were held in abeyance, so if necessary they could be brought to trial later.

It was no surprise that the plea entered by John's assigned counsel was that of not guilty by reason of insanity. Due to his lack of monetary funds, John was unable to hire his own legal team and therefore had to rely on those provided for him. Perhaps this is why his counsel brought forward evidence of all the murders in an attempt to prove he really was insane—a foolish mistake and one that lawyers would not normally make. After all, instead of proving he was insane as they intended, they made the court aware of all of his crimes, which would have clouded any judgement to be made against John's guilt regarding the death of Ethel. A good defense attorney would have tried to get his client off Ethel's murder through circumstances or lack of evidence and kept the rest of the crimes out of it.

To support the plea of insanity, a psychiatrist called Dr. Jack Abbott Hobson was brought before the court as an expert witness for the defense. His testimony included his opinion that John was a severe hysteric, based on his history of hypochondria and the whispering he had continued to demonstrate following the war. He also stated that John likely knew what he was doing when he committed murder but that he did not understand that his actions were wrong. The doctor also believed that John had defective reasoning abilities, rendering him unable to realize how immoral his murderous acts were. However, this last statement was false, as John had the mental capacity to conceal his murders, therefore he must have known his actions were wrong.

Following the doctor's testimony, the prosecution agreed with his diagnosis of John having a hysterical personality, but that this was a neurotic condition and did not affect a person's reasoning abilities. To prove to the court that John had deliberately tried to hide or conceal his crimes, the prosecution submitted the statements John had made to the police during his interrogations where he had tried to be elusive.

Even though he was not legally obligated, John decided to take the stand. Because he had been so successful and convincing while a witness during Timothy Evan's trial, John was super confident about his performance in probing his defense. This was a huge mistake, as the prosecution tore his defense apart. John's manner and composure while on the stand was noticeably agitated and nervous. He fidgeted constantly, clasping and unclasping his hands, tugging at his collar, and running his fingers through his hair. He also sweated profusely, and this is often seen as a sign that the person is guilty or extremely nervous. When a person fears they are about to be found guilty, their heart rate increases, and they sweat more.

Although John had only been charged with the murder of Ethel, the prosecution questioned him about all of the previous known murders John had committed. Unlike many other countries, the British judicial system allows this as a means to prove guilt in the given case at hand. During his testimony, John would regularly fall back to his whispering habits, and he was constantly being told to speak louder.

During the questioning about the other murders, John had said very little regarding the death of Beryl Evans. When he was prodded by the prosecution about her murder, John claimed he had forgotten all about it. This seemed ludicrous to the jury who were aware that John had sat in this vey courtroom and testified against Timothy Evans when he was brought to trial for the murder of Geraldine Evans. This claim by John served to prove to the jury that he was a liar.

The closing argument from the prosecution declared that if John had committed the murders due to insanity, he would have continued to murder without any sense of consequence, meaning that he wouldn't have cared who he killed, where he killed, or if there were any witnesses to the act. With every act of murder John committed, he went to great lengths to hide his actions and any evidence, including the corpses of the murdered. The prosecution showed that John was well aware of the wrongness of what he was doing, and therefore he was indeed sane.

In contrast the closing statement from the defense counsel sought to convince the jurors that any man who could have committed such crimes and continued to live with the bodies of his victims in his own house would have to be insane. They asked the question, what sane man could reasonably carry out such acts and habits? The raping of women as they died, the collecting of pubic hair, and the acts of necrophilia all must be the acts of a mad man.

Conviction and Execution

The judge had instructed the jurors to focus on whether or not John was sane or insane, as this would determine guilt. There was no question in anyone's mind that he had murdered Ethel; the only question was what his state of mind was at the time. The judge himself did not believe the defense had proven insanity, regardless of how abominable his actions had seemed to decent people.

The trial itself had lasted only four days, and the verdict from the jury was also very quick. It took just 85 minutes for the jury to return with a guilty verdict. This resulted in a sentence of death, and in the British legal system that meant the sentence would be carried out very quickly. John had elected to not appeal the sentence, and the date was set for July. Strangely, in Britain there was a condition to death sentences that the prisoner had to be in good health at the time of execution!

Fortunately, or unfortunately depending on how you look at it, John was the picture of good health.

On July 15, 1953, John was led to the Pentonville Prison gallows. Another coincidence that was to occur was that the executioner, Albert Pierrepoint, was the same man who had carried out the execution of Timothy Evans. It seemed that the awful case of Timothy Evans would continue to follow John even to his death.

John was just 54 years old, and complained to Pierrepoint that he had an itchy nose, and because of his bindings he was unable to scratch the itch. Pierrepoint responded with a brilliant comment that it wouldn't be bothering him for long. That was most likely the last thing John heard before he was hanged. Reports stated there were around 200 members of the public stationed outside the prison waiting for news that the execution had been carried out.

Many thought that with the execution of John the story would end there. However, there would be ongoing public interest in John's crimes for a long time to come.

CHAPTER 12:
The Aftermath

Many things took place following the death of John Christie. The area in which John had lived and committed these heinous crimes would be changed forever within the next sixteen years. The admission from him regarding the death of Beryl Evans opened up a lot of questions about the conviction and execution of Timothy Evans, and investigations into this would continue right up until 2004. And there were so many unanswered questions, some of which intrigue people even today.

Demolition of 10 Rillington Place

In 1954, a year after the execution of John, the name of Rillington Place was changed to Ruston Close (also known as Ruston Mews). Those in charge at the time felt that the association between the name of the street and the murders that took place there would stop people from wanting to reside there. However, it wasn't really the street that was the problem, and the number of the house remained the same.

Even so, tenants continued to rent number 10, which is surprising considering it had such a famous and terrible history. How people could live in a flat knowing there had been murders committed there and bodies stored in the pantry is unfathomable. And yet, they continued to come and rent the property right through the 50s, 60s, and into the early 70s.

A film about John's crimes began shooting in 1970, and all current residents of what was now 10 Ruston Close were contacted by the film company, as they wanted to use the property to make the film more authentic. At that time, there were three families living there, and they all refused to move to another property so that filming could be done. Therefore, all of the interior shots were carried out at number 7.

In 1971, it was decided that number 10 should be demolished, and 10 Rillington Place ceased to exist. It was believed, especially following the release of the above-mentioned film, that this would end all association between the location and the murders committed there. This is common practice when there have been horrific murders committed in a house.

Once the house had been destroyed, the area became a residential and light commercial zone, parked between parallel streets called Lancaster Road and Bartle Road. It is difficult to even locate where 10 Rillington Place or any part of Rillington Place had been, and nowadays most people don't know of its previous existence.

Was Timothy Innocent?

Naturally, John Christie confessing to his involvement in the murder of Beryl Evans brought a lot of questions to light regarding the trial of Timothy Evans. As it stood, Timothy had been found guilty of the murder of his daughter, Geraldine, and had hanged for that offense. Although he had never been formally charged for the murder of Beryl, the guilt had been assumed during his trial. Now the public, as well as the legal system, were concerned that Timothy had been sent to his death for a crime he didn't commit.

To investigate this situation, an inquiry was commissioned by the Home Secretary David Maxwell-Fyfe and was led by the Recorder of Portsmouth, John Scott Henderson QC. The sole purpose of this inquiry was to determine whether or not a miscarriage of justice had occurred and that Timothy was innocent. John Christie was interviewed before he went to the gallows, and another twenty witnesses were questioned from each of the police investigations. The conclusion was reached that Timothy had been guilty of the murders of Beryl and Geraldine and that John had lied about his involvement to further enhance his defense argument of insanity.

Despite the inquiry, many felt that it hadn't been fully investigated, and the short duration of eleven days it took to complete the inquiry indicated it had been done in a rush and wasn't thorough enough. There was even suggestion that if both had been guilty, that would mean two stranglers had lived in the very same building at the same time, which would have been incredibly coincidental and therefore not likely. The British Parliament became very involved in this controversy, and many newspapers ran articles declaring an innocent man had been executed. There were even books on the matter written and published almost immediately.

A further inquiry took place during the winter months of 1965-1966. This time, the chair of the inquiry was High Court Judge Sir Daniel Brabin. After going over all of the evidence that had been presented in both cases, and consideration given to the arguments regarding the innocence of Timothy, he reached a conclusion. Brabin believed that Timothy had in fact murdered his wife Beryl, but that he had not killed his baby daughter Geraldine. He determined that John had been guilty of Geraldine's murder, because disposing of her would have prevented questions being asked about the baby, especially if her mother was missing.

Brabin also stated that because of the controversial statements and evidence of the two trials had have been brought to light during a retrial of Timothy, there was very little chance the jury could have been satisfied of reasonable doubt, and Timothy would have been found not guilty of the crime he was being charged with. The Home Secretary at the time of the second inquiry was Roy Jenkins, and Brabin recommended to him that a posthumous pardon be issued for Timothy Evans. On October 18, 1966, the pardon was granted and announced to the House of Commons. By doing so, the family of Timothy were able to reclaim his remains and bury him again in a private grave in St. Patrick's Roman Catholic Cemetery in Leytonstone, instead of the prison cemetery where executed prisoners were interred.

Compensation for the Family

Compensation was granted to the family of Timothy Evans in January 2003 by the Home Office. His half-sister Mary Westlake and full sister Eileen Ashby both received ex gratia payments to compensate for the miscarriage of justice in Timothy's trial and conviction and subsequent hanging. Lord Brennan QC, who was the Home Office's independent assessor, agreed that the conviction and execution of Timothy for the murder of Geraldine was wrongful and that a miscarriage of justice had certainly taken place.

Brennan further stated that there was no evidence that could prove Timothy had murdered his wife Beryl, and that the murder had more likely been carried out by John Christie. John's confessions and statements regarding the murder of Beryl were enough to convince Brennan of his guilt and that the conclusion of the Brabin inquiry should now be rejected.

Mary Westlake went on to try and have Timothy's conviction formally quashed. Although he had received a royal pardon, this did not formally expunge his conviction of murdering Geraldine. Mary started the appeal in the High Court on November 16, 2004. However, the appeal was rejected quickly on the November 19, 2004, as the judges involved considered the resources and costs involved could not be justified by going ahead with the appeal. They did state however that acceptance was given that Timothy was not guilty of the murder of his wife Beryl or his daughter Geraldine.

Judicial Failures Identified

During Brabin's inquiry, a number of issues surrounding malpractice and misconduct by the investigating police were discovered and considered. One of these issues of malpractice was related to the destruction of evidence, including the neck tie that had been used to kill Geraldine, which was destroyed before the other murders committed by John had been discovered. All evidence must be noted in a record book, and this too was destroyed by police. In cases where the charges are serious, especially murders, all evidence and documentation relating to the case must be preserved by the police. It is not known why the police destroyed this evidence, but it was very suspicious.

The numerous statements that had been taken by the police from the accused and witnesses were poorly documented. The way they were written was confusing and many were contradictory. Even the interview dates and times were confused, including those statements taken from John and Ethel Christie during the Timothy Evans case. Those statements supposedly written by Timothy contained language and sentence structure that he simply would not have been capable of.

There were problems with the handling of Timothy Evans while being interviewed by police. Timothy himself had stated that he was coerced and threatened with physical violence by the police to make him confess to the murders of Beryl and Geraldine. It was also thought that Timothy having a very low IQ meant he would have had little understanding of what was being presented to him or what exactly it was he was confessing to. In today's legal system, if a person is borderline mentally retarded, assistance is given to them to ensure they know exactly what is going on.

Naturally the fact that the police failed to notice a human femoral bone propped up against a wooden fence in the backyard of 10 Rillington Place on not one but two occasions had to be questioned. The femur is the largest bone in the human body, more commonly referred to as the thigh bone, and with bleaching from the sun it would most likely to have been quite white in color. How on earth could police officers conducting a scene search at the site of a crime of murder have missed that? If they missed that, what else did they miss?

Brabin tended to prefer the police evidence and did whatever he could to exonerate them of any malpractice or misconduct. He did not investigate the allegations regarding how Timothy was interviewed or the alleged threats made against him. Brabin had little knowledge of forensic evidence and therefore did not consider it important. He also never considered during his inquiry the poor job the police had done in searching the property following the disappearance and subsequent discovery of the bodies of Beryl and Geraldine.

At that period of time, there had already been a lot of discussion and debate throughout the United Kingdom regarding the use of capital punishment. Although there were other controversial cases involving miscarriage of justice at the time, the circumstances surrounding the conviction and execution of Timothy Evans added even more weight to the debate. In 1965, the use of capital punishment was suspended and eventually discontinued completely. No more innocent victims would be hanged for crimes they didn't commit.

CHAPTER 13:
Personality Disorder?

One thing that was known for sure about the mental health and behavior of John Christie was that he was a hypochondriac. From childhood he continued to worry about perceived illnesses he felt he suffered from, but there are no records of him ever really being sick. Apart from the mustard gas exposure during World War I, there had been no further health incidents. Experts who have studied John and his hypochondria also felt that the whispering tendency and temporary muteness he developed, allegedly from the mustard gas, were most likely further signs of his hypochondria.

It can be difficult to understand how a person can do the things John did, especially the sexual activity during the dying minutes of his victims and living in the same house with bodies in the garden, under the floorboards, and in the pantry. Normal, decent people don't do these things, and this led people to believe that he was insane or was suffering from some type of mental illness.

However, as proven during his trial, John was not insane. As hard as that seems to believe, many serial killers are found to be sane at the time of their murderous acts. They know it's wrong and they try to hide their deeds, therefore they are sane and rational. But just because they are sane, it does not mean they are not suffering from some sort of personality disorder.

Narcissistic Personality Disorder

At this point, it must be mentioned that John was never given an actual diagnosis to identify whether he had a personality disorder. But many experts have come to the conclusion after his death that he indeed suffered from a disorder, and one that has been put forward as a diagnosis is Narcissistic Personality Disorder.

A narcissist is one who has a far more elevated sense of their importance than is real, and they need to seek admiration from others. They are not empathetic towards others, and this disorder can cause a lot of issues throughout life, particularly with personal and professional areas. However, behind this behavior is a delicate and low self-esteem, and they can be extremely sensitive to criticism.

People who come into contact with a narcissist often describe them as being pretentious, conceited, and braggarts. Narcissists also tend to take control of conversations in order to be the center of attention. Others are often looked down upon as though they are inferior because the narcissist has such a high sense of importance of themselves. If the narcissist doesn't receive the attention they crave or if their false sense of entitlement isn't met, they can become angry and inpatient.

Along with these feelings of superiority, strangely the narcissist also has feelings of vulnerability, insecurity, humiliation, and shame. This is due to their underlying poor self-esteem, a flaw they do their very best to keep hidden from their peers. The narcissist can fly into a rage to make themselves feel better, or in some cases if they feel as though they are not as perfect as they hoped, they can become depressed. In either case, these behaviors and feelings can deeply affect how they interact with society.

Other symptoms of Narcissistic Personality Disorder can include exaggerating about their achievements in life and what their talents are. They tend to expect that others will recognize just how superior they are even if they haven't done anything to warrant that sort of adoration and respect. John fits this category quite well, claiming he had medical knowledge from his time as a Special Constable and the extreme lengths he took to uphold the law during his time with the War Reserves.

The narcissist displays little or no empathy towards others, which makes them unable to recognize what others are feeling or what their needs are. The ability to kill women and children would be easier because John wouldn't have had a second thought for the victims. All he could focus on was his own needs and wants. However, there was one sign of empathy in the reaction he had to the sentencing and execution of Timothy Evans. Even when John was caught years later, he was still carrying around the newspaper clipping related to the case, and this could have shown some form of guilt on his behalf. He had to have some level of empathy for Timothy, otherwise he wouldn't have shown any interest in the case once he was cleared himself, and he certainly wouldn't have felt any guilt.

Although, during Timothy's court trial, because John was a witness during the trial, his time on the stand would have felt like he was in the limelight. This would have fed John's egotistical sense of himself, and elevated his status in the community—and in his own mind. It's true that many spectators during his testimony believed John to be a good man despite earlier petty crimes, one who had supported his community following the wars and one that was dressed well and spoke well. It just goes to show how a narcissist has the ability to convince and manipulate others to suit their own purposes.

Whether John had Narcissistic Personality Disorder or not is purely conjecture. Obviously in modern day medicine, it's quite possible that he may have been diagnosed with such a disorder. But back in his time, psychiatric medicine wasn't that advanced and so little was known about personality disorders. Besides, it's also possible that John may never have been referred for assessment as a child or an adult. So, we are left with hints and suggestions without rigorous proof. But he certainly does fit the description of the narcissist.

Low Self-Confidence – Due to His Mother?

As mentioned above, narcissists also suffer from poor self-esteem or self-confidence. It's hard to believe really, when you see them placing themselves on a pedestal waiting for recognition and adoration. So where did John's poor self-esteem come from? Could it have been from a father that dished out physical punishment when he saw fit? Or was there more to it?

John's mother was an overbearing and overprotective parent, particularly towards John. His father also used to make the children march on long walks, almost military style. Discipline, routine, and rigidity, were all elements his father brought to the family home. John was considered frail and so his father withdrew from him, unable to tolerate weakness. This opened the door for his mother to create some of the issues he was plagued with for the rest of his life.

Because of his perceived frailty and his father's lack of attention, John's mother took it upon herself to almost smother him with overprotection. John was her favorite child, probably because he was the only boy, and whenever John wanted or needed attention and affection he received it from his mother. This most probably created his hypochondria, as he knew that if he was unwell she would take care of him. It was probably the only time he really got any attention in the household.

Being the only boy in the house also had a detrimental effect on John. Having four sisters older than him, he was clearly outnumbered, and the feminine influence created by so many females in one house would have been strong. His sisters would even dress him up in girls' clothing and treat him like a doll because they thought he was pretty. The girls liked to dominate John, and it is believed that it is the combination of this domination by females and the overprotectiveness of his mother that led or contributed to his hatred of women.

Sexual Dysfunction

John's issues with sexual dysfunction are well documented. As a youth, he had attempted to have intercourse with a girlfriend but was unable to get an erection, and when news of this got out he was ridiculed for many years. He would continue to suffer from impotence throughout his adulthood, and it greatly affected his marriage to Ethel.

Why John was impotent is not entirely clear. However, speculation is that it was because of the dominance he felt from his sisters. From a very young age, he began to see them as sexual objects who both tantalized him sexually then stripped him of his masculinity by treating him like a little girl. This would cause him to love them and hate them all at the same time, and this confusion could have led to the initial problems with impotence.

It wasn't until John was nineteen years old that he discovered he could perform sexual intercourse, but that he could only do so with prostitutes. Even then it didn't always work, and some of the prostitutes used to make fun of him about it or would tell the other girls that he couldn't perform the way a man should.

Again, he was caught in a situation where he loved women and hated them at the same time. Intercourse was probably easier for him with prostitutes because many would let him do whatever he wanted. So if he needed to pretend to strangle the woman during sex, chances are they would allow it for a bit of extra money. Also, he would have perceived prostitutes as being beneath him in social status, feeding his narcissistic tendencies. He wouldn't have had that same feeling with Ethel because she was his wife and therefore his partner, not someone he could treat in the manner he wanted.

John continued to have dalliances with prostitutes throughout his marriage. Whether Ethel knew about it or not is unknown, but it is known that she would frequently go away for periods of time and even left him for a few years. Prostitution was common in London following the wars, as women were left without husbands to support them, and the economy was so poor that they had to do whatever they could to fund a bed for the night or something to eat. Women in particular were desperate creatures post-war, and it was easy for a man like John to take advantage of that.

Perhaps the combination of the female dominance at home, the death of his grandfather, the bullying and ridicule, and his low self-esteem all led to his sexual dysfunction. How exactly John discovered that having intercourse with a woman as she was dying would be so thrilling for him is unknown. One theory is that perhaps while performing erotic asphyxiation with a prostitute (the near-strangulation that some enjoy) the woman died, and this is how he found out it excited him. But we will never really know for sure.

Another theory is that by knocking the women out with the gas, they wouldn't notice if he had issues with gaining an erection and therefore couldn't laugh at him. Or, as a narcissist, their unconsciousness could be associated with submission, and finally he was dominating just as his sisters had dominated him.

Although there are reports that John was a necrophiliac, there was never any proof that he had sex with the bodies after death. He did admit to having sex with them as they were dying, but not after. As mentioned in a previous chapter, this does not mean he wasn't a necrophiliac, as there are varying degrees and types of necrophilia. Stating that one of his victims became fecally and urinary incontinent during sex, and that John had continued to finish the sexual act, he had unwittingly admitted to having sex with a body after death. Also, the bodies in the pantry all had cloths placed between their legs in the same fashion as the woman who had lost control of her bladder and bowels, so perhaps they all had, indicating that he had continued intercourse into the minutes after they had died.

It is extremely important to note here that not all young boys dominated by older sisters grow up to experience the same behavioral and emotional issues that plagued John. Some males are perhaps more predisposed to developing these abnormal personality traits, and little is known about the true cause of why some react differently than others. If John had been alive today, things could have been quite different with the advances in medical and psychiatric studies that simply were not present back then.

CHAPTER 14:
Were There More Victims?

With eight murders already linked to John Christie, people started to look at the patterns of his killing. Most of those murders were sexually motivated, and it's believed that a killer with this type of modus operandi would be highly unlikely to stop or have large gaps between murders. When you put the murders into chronological order, you can see that at one point there was a five year gap. To investigators, theorists, and experts, this is completely out of character for a serial killer. Normally, the only time they stop killing is when they are incarcerated, incapacitated, or dead. None of these situations related to John.

Chronological Murder List

August 1943	Ruth Fuerst
October 1944	Muriel Eady
November 1949	Beryl Evans
November 1949	Geraldine Evans
December 1952	Ethel Christie
January 1953	Rita Nelson

February 1953   Kathleen Maloney

March 1953   Hectorina MacLennan

As you can see, there was more than twelve months between the murder of Ruth Fuerst and Muriel Eady, and then it all comes to a stop for five years. Then, following the murders of Beryl and Geraldine Evans, there was a three year gap before Ethel was killed. Then it all happened rapidly, with a murder being committed every single month in the first three months of 1953.

The gaps between the first five murders led people to question whether or not John had actually committed more murders than what known about. Some even question whether or not he may have committed murder during his military service in World War I. It is unheard of for a serial killer to take such long breaks between kills, and a man such as John, who was sexually motivated to kill, would have continued to have that need all the time, not just every few years.

With his proclivity of sleeping with prostitutes, it's possible that he had killed more women, perhaps in their own rooms. Many of these women would not have been missed by family and loved ones for a number of reasons. They were shunned for taking up the life of prostitution, and in those days they would have been outcast from the family. Therefore, if they were to disappear, it would take a very long time before anybody noticed. This could have provided John with an easy getaway, as he would have had time to distance himself from the prostitute and the crime scene.

Another suspicious aspect was the creation by John of his killing jar, from which he would render his victims into a state of unconsciousness. It seems bizarre to think that he would go to the trouble of creating this murder tool, use it on Muriel Eady, and then not try and use it again for another five years. Then, once he had used it to kill Beryl Evans, he did not use it again for a further two years. With the success of the killing jar, it is incomprehensible that he would have gone for such long periods without using it, especially given his narcissistic tendencies.

Some of the quiet periods could have been related to his wife Ethel. After the murders of Beryl and Geraldine, and John and Ethel being called in as witnesses, perhaps Ethel had her suspicions that her husband was more involved than he claimed. She most likely started to watch his every move, and this could have prevented John from carrying out his dastardly deeds. This would also explain why after Ethel had been disposed of, he went on a rapid-fire killing spree, killing three in three months.

If Ethel had suspected her husband had been involved in the murders of Beryl and her baby daughter, she must have been terrified that the same could happen to her. You may ask why she wouldn't have reported her suspicions to the police, but if they were simply suspicions there was nothing she could have done without proof. Another possibility is that Ethel knew all along what John was doing and she chose to turn a blind eye. Perhaps when she threatened to tell the authorities, he was left with no option but to kill her.

There were calls following John's execution for further investigations into other murders in the area. This was never really carried out, however. London at that time was busy with crime, and police may have felt they had more pressing matters to deal with. Also, they may have had the opinion that John had been executed, and no further legal gains could be made by assigning more murders to him. But, for the families of murder victims, just knowing who had been responsible could have been enough.

But where would you start? His known crimes took place between 1943 and 1953, and ten years of unsolved murders could have been quite substantial. With the possibility of further murders being committed before Ruth Fuerst, or in between the other murders, the scope of potential victims could almost be impossible to gauge. Another consideration is that during his interviews for the murders, John had eluded to the police that perhaps there were others that they did not know about. He never elicited any further information, and because the police hadn't told him they had found the two bodies in the garden, they assumed that those were the murders he thought he'd gotten away with.

The most logical period of time to investigate any unsolved murders and possibly attribute them to John is throughout the 1940's. The environment, the war-time economic situation, and John's love of prostitutes that were plentiful at the time, would all be factors that could have enabled him to murder and go on undetected. There must have been some kind of trigger, and many believe his first murder came about by accident. Another consideration is that perhaps it started during his service in World War I. He was young, sexually dysfunctional, and because of his service would have had a very high opinion of himself, all of which would be contributable to his discovery as murder as a sexual thrill.

There have been cases of killers starting during military service, because as soldiers they are taught to kill without thought or emotion. This could be how the loss of empathy towards victims begins. Not to say that it is to blame, however; there must have been some form of perversion or personality disorder already existent.

Unless someone decides to take on the mammoth task of researching unsolved mysteries in the area John lived during his lifetime, it will never be known if there were more victims than the eight already identified. But it is highly likely that there were indeed many more women who died at John's hands.

Questions Unanswered

Even though John had been convicted, sentenced, and executed, there were still questions that were unanswered and are still not solved today. The deceit John displayed during his police interviews, and the bragging statements he made while incarcerated and awaiting trial, did nothing but provoke even more questions.

John never admitted to killing baby Geraldine Evans. It is assumed he was guilty of this crime, but it was never proven. John may not have wanted to admit to killing the baby, because that would have portrayed him as an even colder and more vicious killer. Just like today, child killers are hated even within prison walls, and he could have been trying to save his own skin. It is certain that Timothy Evans did not kill Geraldine, and that only left John as the potential suspect. Many believe this question is answered by the assumption of guilt, but for others the lack of proof or confession makes this still a mystery.

The Tobacco Tin

Despite John's claims that the collection of pubic hair belonged to his known victims in the house, it was found that just one clump matched Ethel and the rest remained unidentified. This creates a couple of questions—who did the hairs belong to, and why had John kept them? It is possible that two of the clumps may have matched the bodies in the garden, as they were only skeletons when found with no hair samples available. But that still leaves one remaining clump of pubic hair unknown. Some believe that the tin of pubic hair indicates that there were indeed more murders committed by John.

Without knowing who the pubic hair belonged to, it is difficult to surmise why he collected it. Serial killers are known to collect souvenirs, known as 'trophies', from each victim. These are then used to relive the experience of killing the associated victim or, in some cases, just to show themselves how powerful they are that they have been able to commit such a crime, just like hunters that collect animal heads and tails.

Other killers who collect these trophies do so because of a fetish. Perhaps John had a pubic hair fetish, and maybe the prostitutes had willingly given him samples for his collection. There were some women after all that allowed him to take nude photographs of them. So it's clear he had some sort of sexual fantasy going on in his head. England at that time was rather 'proper', and these sorts of behaviors either by the collector or the donor would have been considered perverted. Maybe John liked to keep a memento of his secret life that was so very different from the man he portrayed himself to be.

The collection of pubic hair was obviously very special to John. He kept it preserved in a tobacco tin and kept the tin near him so that he could reach it whenever he wanted—or needed, as the case may be, given his issues with impotence. The collecting of body hair is not unheard of, and more people do it than you probably realize. But not all of these people become serial killers, of course. Looking at the hair, touching it, or smelling it, would have brought back memories of where it came from and from whom, and this was most likely John's motivation for keeping it.

Why Ethel Stayed

Although this question isn't directly related to the murder acts themselves, it must be asked how a woman such as Ethel continued to stand by John until her own death. The marriage can't have been good, given John's sexual dysfunction. While it's true that not everything is about sex, it's an important factor in a marriage, especially if children are wanted. John can't have been able to perform with Ethel, as no children were conceived.

Ethel had left John for quite a long time and then returned following his release from prison for one of his many petty crimes. Why she came back to him nobody knows. It's not like he had a lot to offer her, and with a personality such as his, he can't have been an easy man to live with. But, whatever her reasons, Ethel went back to her marriage and carried on as though she had never left.

The question of Ethel's knowledge about the prostitutes and the murders must also be considered. Although John timed his murders for those times when Ethel was away visiting relatives, surely she must have suspected something was going on, especially after the Evans murders and subsequent trial. Many women in those days stood by their husbands regardless of what they did, as that was what a marriage was supposed to be about back then. You supported and took care of your husband, no matter what—that was your job as a wife.

Unfortunately for Ethel, she really was married until death parted them, by the actions of her husband. Either John had decided she was in the way of his plans to continue killing, or perhaps she had found something out about the murder of Beryl and Geraldine Evans and threated to tell. Nobody will ever know.

CHAPTER 15:
In the Media

The story of John Christie and his terrible murders has been portrayed in a variety of media forms for decades. There have been books, films, and documentaries made, and there are websites out there that are devoted to the tale of John Christie. Listed below are some of the items of media to date.

Movie

10 Rillington Place (1971)

Television

Rillington Place – a three part mini-series due to be released shortly (2016)

Books

John Christie of Rillington Place: Biography of a Serial Killer – Jonathan Oates (2012)

John Christie – Edward Marston (2007)

The Two Killers of Rillington Place – John Eddowes (1995)

The Man on Your Conscience – Michael Eddowes (1955)

Ten Rillington Place – Ludovic Kennedy (1961)

John Christie. Surrey – Edward Marston (2007)

Forty Years of Murder: An Autobiography – Keith Simpson ((1978)

The Two Stranglers of Rillington Place – Rupert Furneaux (1961)

The Trials of Timothy John Evans and John Reginald Halliday Christie – F. Tennyson Jesse (1957)

The Christie Case – Ronald Maxwell (1953)

Reference Items

Rillington Place. London: The Stationery Office – Daniel Brabin (1999)

Medical and Scientific Investigations in the Christie Case – F.E. Camps (1953)

Conclusion

John Christie was clearly a very disturbed yet clever man. To be able to avoid detection for such a long time, even though his flat reeked of decomposing flesh, is remarkable. It is no wonder his case is still being remembered and recognized so many decades later. In fact, there is a new television mini-series set to be released about the case.

The murderous deeds of just one man not only affected those who knew him or were related to the victims, but also led to changes in the street he had lived in and the British judicial system. The house he had committed his murders in was renamed and then completely demolished, and people today struggle to identify where exactly the building stood. Nobody could forget about the bodies that had been hidden there, and so it became necessary to remove that constant reminder.

An innocent man was hanged for a crime that John Christie committed, and although there was a royal pardon, it was far too late for the family of Timothy Evans who were left behind. As late as 2004, they were still trying to seek justice for his wrongful death. The execution of Timothy Evans was partly responsible for Britain removing capital punishment for serious crimes, so no more innocent persons could be sent to the gallows for crimes they did not commit.

Nobody ever suspected John of committing any murders; he was an unassuming although slightly odd man. So clever was his deceit, his wife was seemingly oblivious to what was going on inside her own home. Or maybe she knew, for he would eventually strangle her to death too. People came and went to the flat and noticed the godawful smell, but nobody ever associated it with the stench of a decaying body. Three in the pantry and one under the floor would have made the place reek.

Of course there were also bodies buried in the garden. It is not known why only two victims were buried there and the rest hidden inside the house. His audacity to use a femur from one of the garden victims to prop up a ramshackle wooden fence in the back yard was testament to how sure he was he would never be caught. Regarding the bone, it is simply astounding that on two separate occasions the police searched John's back garden area and not one of them noticed it!

John Christie had seemingly so perfected his method of killing that it is almost impossible to believe that the eight we know about were the only victims. It is highly likely that there were many more women killed by John, and if he hadn't been executed so quickly he may have been convinced to confess.

Unfortunately now, the true tally of his victims will most probably never be known.

The story of John Christie is so perverse and twisted, yet he hid it all so well, that it is disturbing to think these types of people walk among us. As they say, a serial killer is usually the last person you would ever suspect—the neighbor, the man at the bank, or the guy that runs the local dairy. You would never really know what is hidden in their minds and behind their eyes until it is too late. Women didn't fear John—rather they seemed to trust whatever he told them, despite so much of it being lies. They laid in his bed, they followed him home, and nobody ever suspected a thing.

John Reginald Halliday Christie and his dark secrets will forever be known as one of the worst serial killers in British history, and for very good reason.

GET ONE OF MY AUDIOBOOKS FOR FREE

audible
an amazon company

If you haven't joined Audible yet, you can get any
of my audiobooks for FREE!
Find my book on Amazon and click "Buy With Audible Credit"
and you will get the audiobook for FREE!

More books by Jack Rosewood

Among the annals of American serial killers, few were as complex and prolific as Joseph Paul Franklin. At a gangly 5'11, Franklin hardly looked imposing, but once he put a rifle in his hands and an interracial couple in his cross hairs, Joseph Paul Franklin was as deadly as any serial killer. In this true crime story you will learn about how one man turned his hatred into a vocation of murder, which eventually left over twenty people dead across America. Truly, Franklin's story is not only that of a true crime serial killer, but also one of racism in America as he chose Jews, blacks, and especially interracial couples as his victims.

Joseph Paul Franklin's story is unique among serial killers biographies because he gained no sexual satisfaction from his murders and there is no indication that he was ever compelled to kill. But make no mistake about it, by all definitions; Joseph Paul Franklin was a serial killer. In fact, the FBI stated that Franklin was the first known racially motivated serial killer in the United States: he planned to kill as many of his perceived enemies as possible in order to start an epic race war across the country. An examination of Franklin's life will reveal how he became a racially motivated serial killer and the steps he took to carry out his one man war against the world.

Open the pages of this e-book to read a disturbing story of true crime murder in America's heartland. You will be disturbed and perplexed at Franklin's murderous campaign as he made himself a one man death squad, eliminating as many of his political enemies that he could. But you will also be captivated with Franklin's shrewdness and cunning as he avoided the authorities for years while he carried out his diabolical plot!

Richmond, Virginia: On the morning of October 19, 1979, parolee James Briley stood before a judge and vowed to quit the criminal life. That same day, James met with brothers Linwood, Anthony, and 16-year-old neighbor Duncan Meekins. What they planned—and carried out—would make them American serial-killer legends, and reveal to police investigators a 7-month rampage of rape, robbery, and murder exceeding in brutality already documented cases of psychopaths, sociopaths, and sex criminals.

As reported in this book, the Briley gang were responsible for the killing of 11 people (among these, a 5-year-old boy and his pregnant mother), but possibly as many as 20. Unlike most criminals, however, the Briley gang's break-ins and robberies were purely incidental—mere excuses for rape and vicious thrill-kills. When authorities (aided by plea-bargaining Duncan Meekins) discovered the whole truth, even their tough skins crawled. Nothing in Virginian history approached the depravities, many of which were committed within miles of the Briley home, where single father James Sr. padlocked himself into his bedroom every night.

But this true crime story did not end with the arrests and murder convictions of the Briley gang. Linwood, younger brother James, and 6 other Mecklenburg death-row inmates, hatched an incredible plan of trickery and manipulation—and escaped from the "state-of-the-art" facility on May 31, 1984. The biggest death-row break-out in American history.

In the world of American serial killers, few can beat Donald Henry "Peewee" Gaskins when it comes to depravity, cunning, and quite possibly the sheer number of murders. Do not let the nickname "Peewee" fool you, if someone did not take Gaskins seriously, then that person usually ended up dead! In this true crime book about an infamous serial killer, you will delve into the mind of a truly twisted man who claimed scores of victims from the 1950s until 1982, which made him the most prolific serial killer in South Carolina history and quite possibly in all of American history!

Criminal profiling has helped law enforcement capture a number of serial killers throughout history and has also aided mental health professionals understand some of the motives behind their dastardly deeds, but in many ways Gaskins defied most profiles. The range of Gaskins' victims was only equaled by the plethora of reasons he chose to kill: many of the murders were done to appease Gaskins' unnatural carnal desires, while other victims lost their lives during his career as a contract killer. Truly, in the twisted world of psychopaths and sociopaths Gaskins is definitely in the top tier – he was a predator among predators.

Many of the details of Gaskins' life will shock you and still other things will make you horrified by his inhumanity, but in the end you will find that it is impossible to put down this captivating read! So open the book and your mind to see what you will learn in this truly unique serial killer's biography.

This is the true story of the "Meanest Man In America", Donald Henry Gaskins.

GET THESE BOOKS FOR FREE

Go to www.jackrosewood.com

and get these E-Books for free!

FREE BONUS CHAPTER

The making of a serial killer

"I was born with the devil in me," said H.H. Holmes, who in 1893 took advantage of the World's Fair – and the extra room he rented out in his Chicago mansion – to kill at least 27 people without attracting much attention.

"I could not help the fact that I was a murderer, no more than the poet can help the inspiration to sing. I was born with the evil one standing as my sponsor beside the bed where I was ushered into the world, and he has been with me since," Holmes said.

The idea of "I can't help it" is one of the hallmarks of many serial killers, along with an unwillingness to accept responsibility for their actions and a refusal to acknowledge that they themselves used free will to do their dreadful deeds.

"Yes, I did it, but I'm a sick man and can't be judged by the standards of other men," said Juan Corona, who killed 25 migrant workers in California in the late 1960s and early 1970s, burying them in the very fruit orchards where they'd hoped to build a better life for their families.

Dennis Rader, who called himself the BTK Killer (Bind, Torture, Kill) also blamed some unknown facet to his personality, something he called Factor X, for his casual ability to kill one family, then go home to his own, where he was a devoted family man.

"When this monster entered my brain, I will never know, but it is here to stay. How does one cure himself? I can't stop it, the monster goes on, and hurts me as well as society. Maybe you can stop him. I can't," said Rader, who said he realized he was different than the other kids before he entered high school. "I actually think I may be possessed with demons."

But again, he blamed others for not stopping him from making his first murderous move.

"You know, at some point in time, someone should have picked something up from me and identified it," he later said.

Rader was not the only serial killer to place the blame far away from himself.

William Bonin actually took offense when a judge called him "sadistic and guilty of monstrous criminal conduct."

"I don't think he had any right to say that to me," Bonin later whined. "I couldn't help myself. It's not my fault I killed those boys."

It leaves us always asking why

For those of us who are not serial killers, the questions of why and how almost always come to mind, so ill equipped are we to understand the concept of murder on such a vast scale.

"Some nights I'd lie awake asking myself, 'Who the hell is this BTK?'" said FBI profiler John Douglas, who worked the Behavioral Science Unit at Quantico before writing several best-selling books, including "Mindhunter: Inside the FBI's Elite Serial Crime Unit," and "Obsession: The FBI's Legendary Profiler Probes the Psyches of Killers, Rapists, and Stalkers and Their Victims and Tells How to Fight Back."

The questions were never far from his mind - "What makes a guy like this do what he does? What makes him tick?" – and it's the kind of thing that keeps profilers and police up at night, worrying, wondering and waiting for answers that are not always so easily forthcoming.

Another leader into the study of madmen, the late FBI profiler Robert Ressler - who coined the terms serial killer as well as criminal profiling – also spent sleepless nights trying to piece together a portrait of many a killer, something that psychiatrist James Brussel did almost unfailingly well in 1940, when a pipe bomb killer enraged at Con Edison was terrorizing New York City.

(Brussel told police what the killer would be wearing when they arrested him, and although he was caught at home late at night, wearing his pajamas, when police asked him to dress, he emerged from his room wearing a double-breasted suit, exactly as Brussel had predicted.)

"What is this force that takes a hold of a person and pushes them over the edge?" wondered Ressler, who interviewed scores of killers over the course of his illustrious career.

In an effort to infiltrate the minds of serial killers, Douglas and Ressler embarked on a mission to interview some of the most deranged serial killers in the country, starting their journey in California, which "has always had more than its share of weird and spectacular crimes," Douglas said.

In their search for a pattern, they determined that there are essential two types of serial killers: organized and disorganized.

Organized killers

Organized killers were revealed through their crime scenes, which were neat, controlled and meticulous, with effort taken both in the crime and with their victims. Organized killers also take care to leave behind few clues once they're done.

Dean Corll was an organized serial killer. He tortured his victims overnight, carefully collecting blood and bodily fluids on a sheet of plastic before rolling them up and burying them and their possessions, most beneath the floor of a boat shed he'd rented, going there late at night under the cover of darkness.

Disorganized killers

On the flip side of the coin, disorganized killers grab their victims indiscriminately, or act on the spur of the moment, allowing victims to collect evidence beneath their fingernails when they fight back and oftentimes leaving behind numerous clues including weapons.

"The disorganized killer has no idea of, or interest in, the personalities of his victims," Ressler wrote in his book "Whoever Fights Monsters," one of several detailing his work as a criminal profiler. "He does not want to know who they are, and many times takes steps to obliterate their personalities by quickly knocking them unconscious or covering their faces or otherwise disfiguring them."

Cary Stayner – also known as the Yosemite Killer – became a disorganized killer during his last murder, which occurred on the fly when he was unable to resist a pretty park educator.

Lucky for other young women in the picturesque park, he left behind a wide range of clues, including four unmatched tire tracks from his aging 1979 International Scout.

"The crime scene is presumed to reflect the murderer's behavior and personality in much the same way as furnishings reveal the homeowner's character," Douglas and Ressler later wrote, expanding on their findings as they continued their interview sessions.

Serial killers think they're unique – but they're not

Dr. Helen Morrison – a longtime fixture in the study of serial killers who keeps clown killer John Wayne Gacy's brain in her basement (after Gacy's execution she sent the brain away for an analysis that proved it to be completely normal) – said that at their core, most serial killers are essentially the same.

While psychologists still haven't determined the motives behind what drives serial killers to murder, there are certain characteristics they have in common, said Morrison, who has studied or interviewed scores of serial killers and wrote about her experiences in "My Life Among the Serial Killers."

Most often men, serial killers tend to be talkative hypochondriacs who develop a remorseless addiction to the brutality of murder.

Too, they are able to see their victims as inanimate objects, playthings, of you will, around simply for their amusement.

Empathy? Not on your life.

"They have no appreciation for the absolute agony and terror and fear that the victim is demonstrating," said Morrison. "They just see the object in front of them. A serial murderer has no feelings. Serial killers have no motives. They kill only to kill an object."

In doing so, they satisfy their urges, and quiet the tumultuous turmoil inside of them.

"You say to yourself, 'How could anybody do this to another human being?'" Morrison said. "Then you realize they don't see them as humans. To them, it's like pulling the wings off a fly or the legs off a daddy longlegs.... You just want to see what happens. It's the most base experiment."

Nature vs. nurture?

For many serial killers, the desire to kill is as innate at their hair or eye color, and out of control, but most experts say that childhood trauma is an experience shared by them all.

In 1990, Colin Wilson and Donald Seaman conducted a study of serial killers behind bars and found that childhood problems were the most influential factors that led serial killers down their particular path of death and destruction.

Former FBI profiler Robert Ressler – who coined the terms serial killer and criminal profiling – goes so far as to say that 100 percent of all serial killers experienced childhoods that were not filled with happy memories of camping trips or fishing on the lake.

According to Ressler, of all the serial killers he interviewed or studied, each had suffered some form of abuse as a child - either sexual, physical or emotional abuse, neglect or rejection by parents or humiliation, including instances that occurred at school.

For those who are already hovering psychologically on edge due to unfortunate genetics, such events become focal points that drive a killer to act on seemingly insane instincts.

Because there is often no solid family unit – parents are missing or more focused on drugs and alcohol, sexual abuse goes unnoticed, physical abuse is commonplace – the child's development becomes stunted, and they can either develop deep-seeded rage or create for themselves a fantasy world where everything is perfect, and they are essentially the kings of their self-made castle.

That was the world of Jeffrey Dahmer, who recognized his need for control much later, after hours spent in analysis where he learned the impact of a sexual assault as a child as well as his parents' messy, rage-filled divorce.

"After I left the home, that's when I started wanting to create my own little world, where I was the one who had complete control," Dahmer said. "I just took it way too far."

Dahmer's experiences suggest that psychopathic behavior likely develops in childhood, when due to neglect and abuse, children revert to a place of fantasy, a world where the victimization of the child shifts toward others.

"The child becomes sociopathic because the normal development of the concepts of right and wrong and empathy towards others is retarded because the child's emotional and social development occurs within his self-centered fantasies. A person can do no wrong in his own world and the pain of others is of no consequence when the purpose of the fantasy world is to satisfy the needs of one person," according to one expert.

As the lines between fantasy and reality become blurred, fantasies that on their own are harmless become real, and monsters like Dean Corll find themselves strapping young boys down to a wooden board, raping them, torturing them and listening to them scream, treating the act like little more than a dissociative art project that ends in murder.

Going inside the mind: Psychopathy and other mental illnesses

While not all psychopaths are serial killers – many compulsive killers do feel some sense of remorse, such as Green River Killer Gary Ridgeway did when he cried in court after one victim's father offered Ridgeway his forgiveness – those who are, Morrison said, are unable to feel a speck of empathy for their victims.

Their focus is entirely on themselves and the power they are able to assert over others, especially so in the case of a psychopath.

Psychopaths are charming – think Ted Bundy, who had no trouble luring young women into his car by eliciting sympathy with a faked injury – and have the skills to easily manipulate their victims, or in some cases, their accomplices.

Dean Corll was called a Svengali – a name taken from a fictional character in George du Maurier's 1895 novel "Trilby" who seduces, dominates and exploits the main character, a young girl – for being able to enlist the help of several neighborhood boys who procured his youthful male victims without remorse, even when the teens were their friends.

Some specific traits of serial killers, determined through years of profiling, include:

- **Smooth talking but insincere.** Ted Bundy was a charmer, the kind of guy that made it easy for people to be swept into his web. "I liked him immediately, but people like Ted can fool you completely," said Ann Rule, author of the best-selling "Stranger Beside Me," about her experiences with Bundy, a man she considered a friend. "I'd been a cop, had all that psychology — but his mask was perfect. I say that long acquaintance can help you know someone. But you can never be really sure. Scary."

- **Egocentric and grandiose.** Jack the Ripper thought the world of himself, and felt he would outsmart police, so much so that he sent letters taunting the London officers. "Dear Boss," he wrote, "I keep on hearing the police have caught me but they won't fix me just yet. I have laughed when they look so clever and talk about being on the right track. That joke about Leather Apron gave me real fits. I am down on whores and I shan't quit ripping them till I do get buckled. Grand work the last job was. I gave the lady no time to squeal. How can they catch me now? I love my work and want to start again. You will soon hear of me with my funny little games. I saved some of the proper red stuff in a ginger beer bottle over the last job to write with but it went thick like glue and I can't use it. Red ink is fit enough I hope ha. ha. The next job I do I shall clip the lady's ears off and send to the police officers ... My knife's so nice and sharp I want to get to work right away if I get a chance. Good luck."
- **Lack of remorse or guilt.** Joel Rifkin was filled with self-pity after he was convicted of killing and dismembering at least nine women. He called his conviction a tragedy, but later, in prison, he got into an argument with mass murderer Colin Ferguson over whose killing spree was more important, and when Ferguson

taunted him for only killing women, Rifkin said, "Yeah, but I had more victims."

- **Lack of empathy.** Andrei Chikatilo, who feasted on bits of genitalia both male and female after his kills, thought nothing of taking a life, no matter how torturous it was for his victims. "The whole thing - the cries, the blood, the agony - gave me relaxation and a certain pleasure," he said.
- **Deceitful and manipulative.** John Wayne Gacy refused to take responsibility for the 28 boys buried beneath his house, even though he also once said that clowns can get away with murder. "I think after 14 years under truth serum had I committed the crime I would have known it," said the man the neighbors all claimed to like. "There's got to be something that would… would click in my mind. I've had photos of 21 of the victims and I've looked at them all over the years here and I've never recognized anyone of them."
- **Shallow emotions.** German serial killer Rudolph Pliel, convicted of killing 10 people and later took his own life in prison, compared his "hobby" of murder to playing cards, and later told police, "What I did is not such a great harm, with all these surplus women nowadays. Anyway, I had a good time."
- **Impulsive.** Tommy Lynn Sells, who claimed responsibility for dozens of murders throughout the

Midwest and South, saw a woman at a convenience store and followed her home, an impulse he was unable to control. He waited until the house went dark, then "I went into this house. I go to the first bedroom I see...I don't know whose room it is and, and, and, and I start stabbing." The victim was the woman's young son.

- **Poor behavior controls**. "I wished I could stop but I could not. I had no other thrill or happiness," said UK killer Dennis Nilsen, who killed at least 12 young men via strangulation, then bathed and dressed their bodies before disposing of them, often by burning them.

- **Need for excitement.** For Albert Fish - a masochistic killer with a side of sadism that included sending a letter to the mother of one of his victims, describing in detail how he cut, cooked and ate her daughter - even the idea of his own death was one he found particularly thrilling. "Going to the electric chair will be the supreme thrill of my life," he said.

- **Lack of responsibility.** "I see myself more as a victim rather than a perpetrator," said Gacy, in a rare moment of admitting the murders. "I was cheated out of my childhood. I should never have been convicted of anything more serious than running a cemetery without a license. They were just a bunch of worthless little queers and punks."

- **Early behavior problems.** "When I was a boy I never had a friend in the world," said German serial killer Heinrich Pommerencke, who began raping and murdering girls as a teen.
- **Adult antisocial behavior.** Gary Ridgeway pleaded guilty to killing 48 women, mostly prostitutes, who were easy prey and were rarely reported missing – at least not immediately. "I don't believe in man, God nor Devil. I hate the whole damned human race, including myself... I preyed upon the weak, the harmless and the unsuspecting. This lesson I was taught by others: Might makes right."

'I felt like it'

Many psychopaths will say after a crime, "I did it because I felt like it," with a certain element of pride.

That's how BTK killer Dennis Rader felt, and because he had no sense of wrong regarding his actions, he was able to carry on with his normal life with his wife and children with ease.

Someone else's demeanor might have changed, they may have become jittery or anxious, and they would have been caught.

Many serial killers are so cold they are can pop into a diner right after a murder, never showing a sign of what they've done.

"Serial murderers often seem normal," according to the FBI. "They have families and/or a steady job."

"They're so completely ordinary," Morrison added. "That's what gets a lot of victims in trouble."

That normalcy is often what allows perpetrators to get away with their crimes for so long.

Unlike mass murderers such as terrorists who generally drop off the radar before perpetrating their event, serial killers blend in. They might seem a bit strange – neighbors noticed that Ed Gein wasn't too big on personal hygiene, and neighbors did think it was odd that William Bonin hung out with such young boys - but not so much so that anyone would ask too many questions.

"That's why so many people often say, "I had no idea" or "He was such a nice guy" after a friend or neighbor is arrested.

And it's also why people are so very, very stunned when they see stories of serial killers dominating the news.

"For a person with a conscience, Rader's crimes seem hideous, but from his point of view, these are his greatest accomplishments and he is anxious to share all of the wonderful things he has done," said Jack Levin, PhD, director of the Brudnick Center on Violence and Conflict at Northeastern University in Boston and the author of "Extreme Killings."

A new take on psychopathy

Psychopathy is now diagnosed as antisocial personality disorder, a prettier spin on an absolutely horrifying diagnosis.

According to studies, almost 50 percent of men in prison and 21 percent of women in prison have been diagnosed with antisocial personality disorder.

Of serial killers, Ted Bundy (who enjoyed sex with his dead victims), John Wayne Gacy and Charles Manson (who encouraged others to do his dirty work which included the murder of pregnant Sharon Tate) were all diagnosed with this particular affliction, which allowed them to carry out their crimes with total disregard toward others or toward the law.

They showed no remorse.

Schizophrenia

Many known serial killers were later diagnosed with some other form of mental illness, including schizophrenia, believed to be behind the crimes of David Berkowitz (he said his neighbor's dog told him to kill his six victims in the 1970s), Ed Gein, whose grisly saving of skin, bones and various female sex parts was a desperate effort to resurrect his death mother and

Richard Chase (the vampire of Sacramento, who killed six people in California in order to drink their blood).

Schizophrenia includes a wide range of symptoms, ranging from hallucinations and delusions to living in a catatonic state.

Borderline personality disorder

Borderline personality disorder – which is characterized by intense mood swings, problems with interpersonal relationships and impulsive behaviors – is also common in serial killers.

Some diagnosed cases of borderline personality disorder include Aileen Wuornos, a woman whose horrific childhood and numerous sexual assaults led her to murder one of her rapists, after which she spiraled out of control and killed six other men who picked her up along with highway in Florida, nurse Kristen H. Gilbert, who killed four patients at a Virginia hospital with overdoses of epinephrine, and Dahmer, whose murder count rose to 17 before he was caught.

With a stigma still quite present regarding mental illness, it's likely we will continue to diagnose serial killers and mass murderers after the fact, too late to protect their victims.

Top signs of a serial killer

While there is still no simple thread of similarities – which is why police and the FBI have more trouble in real life solving crimes than they do on shows like "Criminal Minds" – there are some things to look for, experts say.

- **Antisocial Behavior.** Psychopaths tend to be loners, so if a child that was once gregarious and outgoing becomes shy and antisocial, this could be an issue. Jeffrey Dahmer was a social, lively child until his parents moved to Ohio for his father's new job. There, he regressed – allegedly after being sexually molested – and began focusing his attentions on dissecting road kill rather than developing friendships.

- **Arson.** Fire is power, and power and control are part of the appeal for serial killers, who enjoy having their victims at their mercy. David Berkowitz was a pyromaniac as a child – his classmates called him Pyro as a nickname, so well-known was he for his fire obsession - and he reportedly started more than 1,000 fires in New York before he became the Son of Sam killer.

- **Torturing animals.** Serial killers often start young, and test boundaries with animals including family or neighborhood pets. According to studies, 70 percent of violent offenders have episodes of animal abuse in their childhood histories, compared to just 6 percent of nonviolent offenders. Albert DeSalvo – better known as the Boston Strangler – would capture cats and dogs as a child and trap them in boxes, shooting arrows at the defenseless animals for sport.

- **A troubled family history.** Many serial killers come from families with criminal or psychiatric histories or alcoholism. Edmund Kemper killed his grandparents to see what it would be like, and later – after he murdered a string of college students – he killed his alcoholic mother, grinding her vocal chords in the garbage disposal in an attempt to erase the sound of her voice.

- **Childhood abuse.** William Bonin – who killed at least 21 boys and young men in violent rapes and murders – was abandoned as a child, sent to live in a group home where he himself was sexually assaulted. The connections suggest either a rage that can't be erased – Aileen Wuornos, a rare female serial killer, was physically and sexually abused throughout her childhood, resulting in distrust of others and a pent-up rage that exploded during a later rape - or a disassociation of sorts, refusing to connect on a human level with others for fear of being rejected yet again.

- **Substance abuse.** Many serial killers use drugs or alcohol. Jeffrey Dahmer was discharged from the Army due to a drinking problem he developed in high school, and he used alcohol to lure his victims to his apartment, where he killed them in a fruitless effort to create a zombie-like sex slave who would never leave him.

- **Voyeurism.** When Ted Bundy was a teen, he spent his nights as a Peeping Tom, hoping to get a glimpse of one of the neighborhood girls getting undressed in their bedrooms.
- **Serial killers are usually smart.** While their IQ is not usually the reason why serial killers elude police for so long, many have very high IQs. Edmund Kemper was thisclose to being considered a genius (his IQ was 136, just four points beneath the 140 mark that earns genius status), and he used his intelligence to create complex cons that got him released from prison early after killing his grandparents, allowing eight more women to die.
- **Can't keep a job.** Serial killers often have trouble staying employed, either because their off-hours activities take up a lot of time (Jeffrey Dahmer hid bodies in his shower, the shower he used every morning before work, because he was killing at such a fast rate) or because their obsessions have them hunting for victims when they should be on the clock.

Trademarks of a serial killer

While what we know helps us get a better understanding of potential serial killers – and perhaps take a closer look at our weird little neighbors – it is still tricky for police and FBI agents to track serial killers down without knowing a few tells.

The signature

While serial killers like to stake a claim over their killings – "Serial killers typically have some sort of a signature," according to Dr. Scott Bonn, a professor at Drew University in New Jersey – they are usually still quite neat, and a signature does not necessarily mean evidence.

"Jack the Ripper, of course, his signature was the ripping of the bodies," said Bonn.

While there are multiple theories, Jack the Ripper has yet to be identified, despite the similarities in his murders.

Too, the Happy Face Killer, Keith Hunter Jespersen – whose childhood was marked by alcoholic parents, teasing at school and a propensity to abuse small animals - drew happy faces on the numerous letters he sent to both media and authorities, teasing them a bit with a carrot on a string.

"If the forensic evidence itself - depending upon the bones or flesh or whatever is left - if it allows for that sort of identification, that would be one way of using forensic evidence to link these murders," Bonn said.

The cooling off period

Organized killers are so neat, tidy and meticulous that they may never leave clues, even if they have a signature.

And if there's a long cooling off period between crimes, tracking the killer becomes even more of a challenge.

After a murder – which could be compared to a sexual experience or getting high on drugs – the uncontrollable urges that led the killer to act dissipate, at least temporarily.

But according to Ressler, serial killers are rarely satisfied with their kills, and each one increases desire – in the same way a porn addiction can start with the pages of Playboy then turn into BDSM videos or other fetishes when Playboy pictorials are no longer satisfying.

"I was literally singing to myself on my way home, after the killing. The tension, the desire to kill a woman had built up in such explosive proportions that when I finally pulled the trigger, all the pressures, all the tensions, all the hatred, had just vanished, dissipated, but only for a short time," said David Berkowitz, better known as the Son of Sam.

Afterwards, the memory of the murder, or mementos from the murder such as the skulls Jeffrey Dahmer retained, the scalps collected by David Gore or the box of vulvas Ed Gein kept in his kitchen, no longer become enough, and the killers must kill again, creating a "serial" cycle.

That window between crimes usually becomes smaller, however, which allows authorities to notice similarities in murder scenes or methodology, making tracking easier.

In the case of William Bonin, there were months between his first few murders, but toward the end, he sometimes killed two young men a day to satisfy his increasingly uncontrollable urges.

"Sometimes... I'd get tense and think I was gonna go crazy if I couldn't get some release, like my head would explode. So I'd go out hunting. Killing helped me... It was like ... needing to go gambling or getting drunk. I had to do it," Bonin said.

Hunting in pairs

Some serial killers – between 10 and 25 percent - find working as a team more efficient, and they use their charm as the hook to lure in accomplices.

Ed Gein may never have killed anyone had his accomplice, a mentally challenged man who helped Gein dig up the graves of women who resembled his mother, not been sent to a nursing home, leaving Gein unable to dig up the dead on his own.

Texas killer Dean Corll used beer, drugs, money and candy to bribe neighborhood boys to bring him their friends for what they were promised was a party, but instead would turn to torture and murder. He would have killed many more if one of his accomplices had not finally shot him to prevent another night of death.

William Bonin also liked to work with friends, and he enticed boys who were reportedly on the low end of the IQ scale to help him sadistically rape and torture his victims.

Other red flags

According to the FBI's Behavioral Science Unit – founded by Robert Ressler - 60 percent of murderers whose crimes involved sex were childhood bed wetters, and sometimes carried the habit into adulthood. One such serial killer, Alton Coleman, regularly wet his pants, earning the humiliating nickname "Pissy."

Sexual arousal over violent fantasies during puberty can also play a role in a serial killer's future.

Jeffrey Dahmer hit puberty about the same time he was dissecting road kill, so in some way, his wires became crossed and twisted, and sex and death aroused him.

Brain damage? Maybe

While Helen Morrison's test found that John Wayne Gacy's brain was normal, and Jeffrey Dahmer's father never had the opportunity to have his son's brain studied, although both he and Jeffrey had wanted the study, there is some evidence that some serial killers have brain damage that impact their ability to exact rational control.

"Normal parents? Normal brains? I think not," said Dr. Jonathan Pincus, a neurologist and author of the book "Base Instincts: What Makes Killers Kill."

"Abusive experiences, mental illnesses and neurological deficits interplayed to produce the tragedies reported in the newspapers. The most vicious criminals have also been, overwhelmingly, people who have been grotesquely abused as children and have paranoid patterns of thinking," said Pincus in his book, adding that childhood traumas can impact the developmental anatomy and functioning of the brain.

***

So what do we know?

Serial killers can be either uber-smart or brain damaged, completely people savvy or totally awkward, high functioning and seemingly normal or unable to hold down a job.

But essentially, no matter what their back story, their modus operandi or their style, "they're evil," said criminal profiler Pat Brown.

And do we need to know anything more than that?

A Note From The Author

Hello, this is Jack Rosewood. Thank you for reading this true crime story. I hope you enjoyed the read of this chilling story. If you did, I'd appreciate if you would take a few moments to post a review on Amazon.

I would also love if you'd sign up to my newsletter to receive updates on new releases, promotions and a FREE copy of my Herbert Mullin E-Book, www.jackrosewood.com

Thanks again for reading this book, make sure to follow me on Facebook.

A big thanks to Rebecca Lo who helped me write this book.

Best Regards
Jack Rosewood

Printed in Great Britain
by Amazon